POWER
OF KIND
WORDS

WINNING WITH KIND WORDS

THE
POWER
OF KIND
WORDS

WINNING WITH KIND WORDS

MICHAEL ATUNRASE, SR.

ISBN: 978-0997520019
For information contact; address

MOLAT PUBLISHERS
2660 Trenton Road,
Levittown, PA 19056
Email: 7Realitiesdaily@gmail.com

@Bishopmichaelatunrase

DEDICATION

*To my mother Emily-Mabel, who was
an example of a kind soul.
To my loving wife, Lola.
To Michael Jr. and Jacqueline, Emily-Rachael,
Sarah-Elizabeth, Joshua-Emmanuel and
grandchildren Ava-Jade, Michael-James
our beloved children.*

*And to all who believe that through kindness
our world can be a better place.*

ACKNOWLEDGEMENTS

I do acknowledge the grace of God and the privilege to share the message of this book. Also, I would like to thank everyone who made this project possible.

Thank you to Minister Carol Di Santo for your excellent editorial assistance.

CONTENTS

PREFACE

The Power of Kind Words

On July 23, 2018, a trailer had a flat tire and its rim scraped the asphalt causing sparks that started what is now one of the largest wildfires in the history of the state of California. The fire blazed a fiery trail along the highway, burning up dry brush and residential areas, leaving several dead, displacing countless number of people from their homes and leaving neighborhoods in piles of ashes.

What an unbearable burden it must have been for the couple whose trailer started this fire to see the vast devastation caused by their unfortunate incident. However, the people of this Northern California community did something wonderfully heroic. They sent this message to the couple: *"It's not your fault."* What a great relief it was for this couple to hear such unexpected but kind words, and how liberating it must have been for them to receive such encouragement from those who had lost their homes and fortunes in this wildfire.

A CNN correspondent wrote about the incident:
When Redding resident, Rachel Pilli read about the tire failure, she decided to reach out to the trailer's owners with a message of compassion. She posted a message on social media asking if anyone else wanted to show their support. About 100 letters poured in -- and they're still coming.

"I was thinking if I could send a card, maybe my friends would also send a card," Pilli told CNN affiliate KRCR. Her plea for a supportive message was shared on a Facebook page called Carr Fire Stories, where the page's administrator said more than 300 people responded. "We had firefighters out there fighting the fire send notes, we've had counselors saying they would be willing to meet with the couple, we've had people who've lost everything, and they are even saying, *"It's not your fault,"* **(Faith Karimi, CNN, Wed. August 15, 2018).**

INTRODUCTION

IN ANY OF YOUR RELATIONSHIPS, your words will determine whether you lose your friends or make new enemies, but kind words will help you keep your friends or win over your enemies. As oil fuels the fire and water, on the other hand kills the fire, your words will either enhance or damage your relationships. Kind words have the power to inspire others; uplifting words can replace the feelings of low self-esteem with a healthy sense of self-worth, kind words can cause people to breakthrough into new levels of possibilities.

It is amazing what positive affirmation can produce in the life of a little child. If you speak some kind words to someone today, even to a child, you may never know how much good it can bring into that life. Try it, it will cost you nothing, but it might mean all the world to the person you spoke them to.

"One word or a pleasing smile is often enough to raise up a saddened and wounded soul." St. Teresa of Lisieux.

Circumstances and discretion will suggest when it is necessary to be stern with critics or the opposition, at the time, it will be a matter of principles and not a matter of lapse in character.

We understand according to Scriptures, that God created the light and the firmaments by His Word, and that the worlds were framed by the Word of God (Genesis 1:3, Hebrews 11:2). God used the spoken word to create both the material and the immaterial world. It is apparent then that spoken words possess spiritual properties and have the power to create or birth our thoughts and desires. Since we were created in the image of God, we also possess power in our words, so that our words affect the world around us, can change our circumstances and even affect nature.

A stimulus (force) is required for a change to occur in any dimension; whether in the physical, spiritual, mental or emotional realms. The spoken word is a stimulus and possess the power to effect change in any of these realms.

A person's behavior or attitude is an index of several character traits that make up their whole personality. Speaking kind and unpretentious words reflect a person's character. Kindness, loyalty, sincerity and devotion are all good character traits and they reflect a beautiful nature. Jesus said,

> "43For a good tree does not bear bad fruit, nor does a bad tree bear good fruit. 44For every tree is known by its own fruit. For men do not gather figs from thorns, nor do they gather grapes from a bramble bush. 45*A good man out of the good treasure of his heart brings forth good; and an evil man out of the evil treasure of his heart brings forth evil. For out of the abundance of the heart his mouth speaks*" (Luke 6:43-45).

The Impact of Kind Words

CHAPTER 1

*"Kind words are like honey, sweet
to the soul and healthy for the body"*
(Proverbs 16:24 NLT).

WORDS HAVE POWER to encourage or discourage, inspire or dampen the spirit. It is a sobering thought that you can change someone's day or greatly impact their future by your words, therefore be watchful of your words to others. You have heard it said, *"If you cannot be kind, then be quite."*

> **"Anxiety in the heart of man causes depression, but a good word makes it glad" (Proverbs 12:25).**

Let me share a true story with you:

I had a very big family as a young boy. I remember many of my uncles and aunties, but out of them all one uncle stood out, Uncle James. He was kind, gentle and a successful medical practitioner. I remembered that he was always glad to see me whenever I went by his house. I greatly admired him for being a kindhearted and giving person; he was my childhood hero. One day while visiting with him, he said to me, "You know, you would make a good doctor, if you face your studies." I was only nine years old and those words meant a lot to me and set me on a course to pursue a medical career.

When it was time to start medical school, I was called into the Christian ministry. Though I was disappointed that I had prepared all these years for this moment, on the other hand I was glad that God was calling me to be His minister and answering my mother's prayers of many years that God would make me His servant. I have been away from home for many years now, and after twenty long years, I had the opportunity to see my uncle again. He was now old and

13

retired from his medical practice. I did have some reservations and experienced some feelings of regret as I anticipated our meeting. I knew that he was aware that I am not a doctor but a Christian minister, though I had travelled abroad to pursue medical training.

As we reminisced about old times, he said, "I heard that you are now in full-time ministry as a pastor," and I said, "yes sir!" I continued to say, "You know I wanted to be a doctor like you," to which he replied, "Yes, but I am pleased that God called you to a more noble profession than you wanted." "I am glad there is a minister of God in our family. It is better to be a minister of God, than to be a minister of the state." I cannot tell you how much those words mean to me, especially coming from him, the one I greatly admired and wanted to be like. He told me that God chose a better path for me. And before I left him, he asked, "Pastor would you pray for me," and I had the opportunity to pray with him. It was a memorable moment for me.

My uncle died a few years after that meeting. I was grateful to have seen him again and to have closure to something that was very important to me. Twice his kind words made a great impact in my life, once as a 9-year-old boy and later as a 45-year-old man. You never know what impact kind words can have on others, especially in the life of a child.

> *"Your words have put stumbling people on their feet, put **fresh hope** in people about to collapse"* **(Job 4:4 MSG-The Message).**

Indeed, it's remarkable what positive words can do for the psyche. Watch a person's face light up when you extend a compliment, no matter how deep or superficial. Mother Teresa once said, *"Kind words are short and easy to speak, but their echoes are truly endless."*

Speaking Kind Words is Kindness

The reason why some find it difficult to speak kind words is because they are not kindhearted. Kind and unpretentious words come from kind hearts; it is impossible to separate the two. Speaking kind words is kindness and kind words are always right words.

> *"A good man out of the good treasure of his heart brings forth good; and an evil man out of the evil treasure of his heart brings forth evil. For out of the abundance of the heart his mouth speaks"* **(Luke 6:45).**

Communicating Kind Words

Generally, communication can take any of three methods, spoken, written, and signed (sign language). Therefore, people communicate kind words in these different ways.

Verbal Communication: The use of words to express or communicate a message. The two forms of verbal communication are the written and oral communication.

Written Communication: The use of written words, i.e., letters, emails, chat texts, SMS, social media (i.e., Facebook) or any symbolic language.

Oral Communication: This uses the spoken word, either face-to-face, via telephone, video conferencing, voice chats, TV, etc.

Non-Verbal Communication: The use of wordless messages to convey the message as in the use of body language (i.e., facial expressions) and sign language.

Visual Communication: This is another kind of non-verbal communication, and this employs the use of visual aids; such as signs, color, illustration and graphic designs to communicate the message.

Kindness Has No Limits

For years scientists and emotion researchers have wondered if there is proof that animals are capable of empathy. There is increasing evidence mostly in mammals and in birds that show that animals are sensitive to emotional reactions and can detect distress signals in others, and attempt to comfort and even rescue fellow animals from dangers.

There are stories of animals (lions, elephants, birds, and monkeys) who respond affectionately to people who were kind to them whenever they reunite again after many years. There was a case of a lion who remembered the man who rescued and nurtured her while she was just a little cub after eight years.

A video from India shows a monkey saving the life of another monkey that had fallen unconscious onto the train tracks after it was electrocuted. This monkey is seen attempting what seems to be a resuscitation technique, by repeatedly biting, hitting, flipping, and dipping the unconscious monkey in water, until the unconscious monkey revived after twenty minutes. This video and many others like it shows the undeniable proof of empathy in animals. Kindness and compassion involves understanding and responding empathetically to the needs and desires of others. It was the most amazing sight to see this display of empathy (kindness) in this animal.

Kindness seems to be an emotional reaction that is possible in most animals and if animals understand this on their level and can respond with empathy to another in need, this might suggest that being unkind is unnatural for humans. Can we learn from the animals? Yes! We are instructed several times in Scriptures to learn from animals and to observe the rest of nature. Isn't this what we call science?

> "7But now ask **the beasts**, and they **will teach you;** and **the birds of the air,** and they **will tell you;** 8or speak to **the earth,** and it **will teach you;** and **the fish** of the sea **will explain to you.** 9 **Who among all these does not know that the hand of the Lord has done this,** 10 in whose hand is the life of every living thing, and the breath of all mankind?" **(Job 12:7-10).**

One of the great attributes of the Creator-God is His loving-kindness, it is not surprising that uncorrupted nature can reflect this divine attribute.

> "3At one time we too were foolish, disobedient, deceived and enslaved by all kinds of passions and pleasures. We lived in malice and envy, being hated and hating one

17

another. **⁴ But when the kindness and love of God our Savior appeared**, *⁵ he saved us, not because of righteous things we had done, but because of his mercy. He saved us through the washing of rebirth and renewal by the Holy Spirit, ⁶ whom he poured out on us generously through Jesus Christ our Savior"* **(Titus 3:3-6 NIV).**

Breaking Barriers Through Kindness

"Kindness is the language which the deaf can hear and the blind can see." **Mark Twain**

A YouTube video featured a story of a deaf man Muharrem, from Istanbul, who was moved to tears after learning that his neighborhood had learned sign language just for him to promote the message: *"A world without barriers is our dream,"* sponsored by Samsung. A team of people from Samsung and an ad agency spent a month secretly setting up cameras and teaching people sign language throughout Muharrem's neighborhood.

Muharrem sets out on a typical day with his sister, Ozlem, on a routine walk to the local shops, but unknown to him, he was being secretly filmed. They met with strangers (actors who were in on the stunt), who for this purpose had learned sign language.

The first encounter was meeting a stranger who signed "good morning" to him. And more surprisingly, was his visit to his local food store where the shopkeeper offers him a "hot bagel" through hand signals. Next, was a stranger who accidentally dropped his bags of fruit and as Muharrem and his sister helped the man pick up the apples, the man signed to offer them both apples as a thank you. He was shocked as the man signed to him, and asked his sister if she knew the man and if the man was hearing impaired.

He hardly had time to take in all that was happening; it felt odd that everyone so far had been signing to him today. Just then a lady bumps into him accidentally and right away signed, "Sorry, my mistake." They waved down a taxi and again he was completely stunned as the taxi driver greeted and welcomed him in the car with sign language.

And finally, as they came to the city square, there was an electronic advertising board set up to communicate these kind words to him, **"Hi, Muharrem, at Samsung we wanted to prepare a little surprise for you because, a world without barriers is our dream as well."** A friend finally points Muharrem to several of the hidden cameras, bringing him to tears. The purpose of this commercial by Samsung was to promote its new video call centers for the hearing impaired. Since being posted to YouTube, the video has been viewed thirteen million, eight-hundred thousand times as of March 2016.

You can view the heartwarming video here: https://www.youtube.com/watch?v=UrvaSqN76h4

Abraham Lincoln

Despite his busy schedule during the Civil War, Abraham Lincoln often visited the hospitals to cheer the wounded. On one occasion he saw a young fellow who was near death. "Is there anything I can do for you?" asked the compassionate President.

"Please write a letter to my mother," came the reply. Unrecognized by the soldier, the Chief Executive sat down and wrote as the youth told him what to say.

The letter read, "My Dearest Mother, I was badly hurt while doing my duty, and I won't recover. Don't sorrow too much for me. May God bless you and Father. Kiss Mary and John for me." The young man was too weak to go on, so Lincoln signed the letter for him and then added this postscript: "Written for your son by Abraham Lincoln."

Asking to see the note, the soldier was astonished to discover who had shown him such kindness. "Are you really our President?" he asked. "Yes," was the quiet answer. "Now, is there anything else I can do?" The lad feebly replied, "Will you please hold my hand? I think it would help to see me through to the end." The tall, gaunt man granted his request, offering warm words of encouragement until death stole in with the dawn.
Source unknown.

The Power of Kind Words

Kathy Whirity shares a true story about Ophrah Winfrey's childhood, she writes:

> "A recent topic on the Oprah show had a simple concept that left me wondering why, since it is so obviously positive, more people aren't practicing the art of passing along kind words.
>
> On this show, Oprah was completely taken off guard when a woman from her childhood made a surprise appearance. Clearly it was an emotional moment for the queen of television who explained,

through tears, how this woman's kind words of long ago, greatly impacted her life. As Oprah tells it, she was about 8 years old when this woman, whom she had never met, looked at her and said: "You are as cute as a speckled pup." Though Oprah didn't quite know what she really meant, she knew it was a compliment and that single remark helped to empower an otherwise timorous child to begin to believe in herself. The phenomenally successful Oprah Winfrey stood on the stage of her enormously popular talk show with this lady, tears streaming down her face as the emotional impact of four decades ago still holds meaning that causes a stirring in her soul."

5But I would strengthen you with my mouth, And the comfort of my lips would relieve your grief' **(Job 16:2-5).**

John Trent wrote a touching story to illustrate the impact of words:

"Mary had grown up knowing that she was different from the other kids, and she hated it. She was born with a cleft palate and had to bear the jokes and stares of cruel children who teased her non-stop about her misshaped lip, crooked nose, and garbled speech. With all the teasing, Mary grew up hating the fact that she was "different." She was convinced that no one, outside her family, could ever love her … until she entered Mrs. Leonard's class.

Mrs. Leonard had a warm smile, a round face, and shiny brown hair. While everyone in her class liked her, Mary came to love Mrs. Leonard. In the 1950's, it was common for teachers to give their children an annual hearing test. However, in Mary's case, in addition to her cleft palate, she was barely able to hear out of one ear. Determined not to let the other children have another "difference" to point out, she would cheat on the test each year. The "whisper test" was given by having a child walk to the classroom door, turn sideways, close one ear with a finger, and then repeat something which the teacher whispered. Mary turned her bad ear towards her teacher and pretended to cover her good ear. She knew that teachers would often say things like, 'The sky is blue,' or 'What color are your shoes?'

But not on that day. Surely, God put seven words in Mrs. Leonard's mouth that changed Mary's life forever. When the "whisper test" came, Mary heard the words: 'I wish you were my little girl.' Dads, I wish there was some way that I could communicate to you the incredible blessing which affirming words impart to children. I wish too, that you could sit in my office, when I counsel, and hear the terrible damage that individuals received from not hearing affirming words -- particularly affirming words from a father. While words from a godly teacher can melt a heart, words from a father can powerfully set the course of a life.

If affirming words were something rarely spoken in your home growing up, let me give you some tips on words and phrases that can brighten your own child's eyes and life. These words are easy to say to any child who comes into your life: I'm proud of you, Way to go, Bingo … you did it, Magnificent, I knew you could do it, What a good helper, You're very special to me, I trust you, What a treasure, Hurray for you, Beautiful work, You're a real trooper, Well done, That's so creative, You make my day, You're a joy, Give me a big hug, You're such a good listener, You figured it out, I love you, You're so responsible, You remembered, You're the best, You sure tried hard, I've got to hand it to you, I couldn't be prouder of you, You light up my day, I'm praying for you, You're

wonderful, I'm behind you, You're so kind to your (brother/sister), You're God's special gift, I'm here for you."
(John Trent, Ph.D., Vice President of Today's Family, *Men of Action,* **Winter 1993, p. 5).**

The Power of Kind Criticism

Constructive criticism is tough to give, criticism does not always land well. It is often a difficult conversation for the giver and can trigger undesirable reactions in the receiver. However, criticism expressed with kindness may receive attention and in turn bring amazing results. King Solomon remarked on the value of a kind critic. *"Like an earring of gold and an ornament of fine gold, is **a wise reprover** to an ear that listens and learns"* (Proverbs 25:12 AMP-Amplified Bible). Paul the Apostle also said to *"speak the truth in love."* Try to be an encourager; the world has too many critics already.

CRITICISM EXPRESSED WITH KINDNESS MAY RECEIVE ATTENTION AND IN TURN BRING AMAZING RESULTS

"but speaking the truth in love, ..."
(Ephesians 4:15a).
Kind or Constructive Criticism:

- Avoids being insulting to the receiver, rather it's focus is on pointing out how the receiver can do better.
- Provides recommendations and examples on how to do better.

- Employs the idea of praising in public but criticizing only in private; people appreciate not being publicly criticized.

"Like apples of gold in settings of silver is a word spoken in right circumstances" **(Proverbs 25:11 NASB-New American Standard Bible).**

The following story illustrates the power of kind criticism:

Graeme McDowell, a professional golfer was preparing for the 2006 British Open Championship. On the eve of this great tournament, he still wasn't quite sure what it was that was not perfect about his play. While he was out for the evening, McDowell met with a surprise. A stranger who was an avid golf fan, recognized him and commented that he had noticed a flaw in his swing. The next day, Graeme tested that advice on the driving range, and to his great shock he discovered that the fan had been correct. Satisfied with the value of the change, Graeme implemented the suggestion and finished the first day of the British Open in first place! All because a stranger took time to speak a word of help.

The Impact of Kind Words

"Drop a pebble in the water,
splash, and it is gone;
but there's half-a-hundred ripples
circling on and on and on.
Spreading, spreading
from the center to the sea,
and there is no way of telling
where the end is going to be."

"Drop an unkind word, or careless,
a minute and it's gone,
but there's half-a-hundred ripples
circling on and on and on.
Spreading, spreading,
from the center as they go,
for there is no way to stop them
once you've started them to flow."

"Drop a word of cheer and kindness,
flash and it is gone,
but there's half-a-hundred ripples
circling on and on and on.
Bearing hope and comfort
on each splashing, dashing wave
'till you wouldn't believe the volume
of the one kind word you gave."
- Kristi Rieger Campbell.

The Mutual Benefit
of Speaking Kind Words

CHAPTER 2

*"A man has joy by the answer of his mouth,
and a word spoken in due season,
how good it is!"* (Proverbs 15:23).

I T IS TRUE THAT KIND WORDS have reciprocal effect, as when you spray perfume well enough on someone else, you are bound to have some on yourself. When we speak kind words to others, it lights up their faces and brings them joy and in turn, we share in the seed of joy we have sown. The old wise king once said,

> *"A man has joy by the answer of his mouth, and a word spoken in due season, how good it is!"* **(Proverbs 15:23).**

A man derives joy by what he says to others. Kind words are intentional, they are like custom-made jewelry carefully crafted for the recipient.

> *"The right word at the right time is like a custom-made piece of jewelry"* **(Proverbs 25:11 MSG).**

The relationship experts all agree that the most critical need in any relationship is communication and that whenever there has been problems in relationships, it is always traceable not only to lack of communication but also to bad communication. People often wonder how their relationship became bad but forget to note that it began when they stopped caring about their words. When people become careless about their words and begin to speak unkind words to their friends, spouse, bosses,

> PEOPLE OFTEN WONDER HOW THEIR RELATIONSHIPS BECAME BAD, BUT FORGET TO NOTE THAT IT BEGAN WHEN THEY STOPPED CARING ABOUT THEIR WORDS

business partners, and customers, the relationship starts to degrade at that moment.

The following article once appeared in a U.S. News & World Report:

> "In order to uncover the processes that destroy unions, marital researchers study couples over the course of years, and even decades, and retrace the star-crossed steps of those who have split up back to their wedding day. What they are discovering is unsettling. None of the factors that one would guess might predict a couple's durability actually does not how in love a newlywed couple say they are; how much affection they exchange; how much they fight or what they fight about. In fact, couples who will endure and those who won't look remarkably similar in the early days.
>
> Yet when psychologists Cliff Notarius of Catholic University and Howard Markman of the University of Denver studied newlyweds over the first decade of marriage, they found a very subtle but telling difference at the beginning of the relationships. Among couples who would ultimately stay together, 5 out of every 100 comments made about each other were putdowns. Among couples who would later split, 10 of every 100 comments were insults. That gap magnified over the following decade, until couples heading downhill were flinging five times as many cruel and invalidating comments at each other as happy couples.
>
> "Hostile putdowns act as cancerous cells that, if unchecked, erode the relationship over time," says Notarius, who with Markman co-authored the new book 'We Can Work It Out'. "In the end, relentless unremitting negativity takes control and the couple

can't get through a week without major blowups." **(U.S. News & World Report, February 21, 1994, Page 6).**

The Prince Who Lost Most of His Kingdom

Rehoboam was the son of Solomon the famous King of Israel. After the king's death, Rehoboam became the new king. The transition wasn't as smooth as it could have been, because there were some problems carried over from the reign of Solomon, his father. King Solomon was unusually favored by God and as a result, became very great. But then he took on many wives who turned his heart from the Lord his God.

And because of his continuous idolatry, he fell out of favor with God. So, God sent a message with the prophet Ahijah to Jeroboam, one of King Solomon's servant, to inform him that God was choosing him as king to rule over ten of the tribes of Israel, and that God would allow just one tribe to remain in the hand of Rehoboam for King David's sake. When King Solomon heard of Jeroboams' prospect, he attempted to execute him, but Jeroboam fled to Egypt until the death of King Solomon.

> *"**Solomon therefore sought to kill Jeroboam.** But Jeroboam arose and fled to Egypt, to Shishak king of Egypt, and was in Egypt until the death of Solomon"* **(1 Kings 11:40).**

After King Solomon's death, his son Rehoboam, became king and Jeroboam returned from Egypt by popular demand. Jeroboam and the people came to their new king to plead with him to reconsider his father's policy of excessive taxation and forced labor and in return, they promised the king their service and loyalty.

> *"Through patience a ruler can be persuaded, and a gentle tongue can break a bone"* **(Proverbs 25:15 NIV).**

The king asked for three days to reply to the people's request and went to ask for advice from the elders of the land, who were experienced statesmen and the king's privy councilors. This seemed to be the only thing the young king did right in the whole story. It was a nice gesture that he consulted with the elders, but he could have taken to his own father's counsel as written in the Book of Proverbs.

> *"Trust God from the bottom of your heart; don't try to figure out everything on your own. Listen for God's voice in everything you do, everywhere you go; he's the one who will keep you on track. Don't assume that you know it all. Run to God! Run from evil!"* **(Proverbs 3:5-7 MSG).**

The king's counsellors advised the young king in this manner:

> *"And they spoke to him, saying,* **"If you are kind to these people,** *and please them,* **and speak good words** *to them, they will be your servants forever"* **(2 Chronicles 10:7).**

The elders believed that kindness is the key to winning people's hearts, that it was best to respond to the people with kind consideration and assuring words. Solomon, the king's father once said,

"A soft answer turns away wrath, but a harsh word stirs up anger" (**Proverbs 15:1**).

These aged senators could discern that it was a critical time in Israel and that the king needed to be sensitive to the people. It was no time to flex royal muscles or be unreasonable.

Though Jeroboam had been promised rulership over most of the nation, he was here now with the people pleading for the king's favor and pledging his loyalty and service to the king.

> KINDNESS IS THE KEY TO WINNING PEOPLES HEART

One wonders what might have been, or what could have happened if the king had granted the people's request! Is it possible that the king could have won Jeroboam's heart along with all Israel, only if he had spoken kind words?

The king seemed not to have been satisfied with the advice of the elders. Instead, he rejected the counsel of the elders and went to his peers (the young men) who had grown up with him, and this is what they advised him:

> *"10 Then the young men who had grown up with him spoke to him, saying, "Thus you should speak to this people who have spoken to you, saying, 'Your father made our yoke heavy, but you make it lighter on us' — thus you shall say to them: 'My little finger shall be thicker than my father's waist! 11 And now, whereas my father put a heavy yoke on you, I will add to your yoke; my father chastised you with whips, but I will chastise you with scourges"* (**2 Chronicles 10:10-11**).

It is not to say that young men cannot give sound advice nor true that old men always give good advice, but the advantage of experience is knowledge.

The Advantage of Experience Is Knowledge

"Those [who are] abundant in years may not [always] be wise, nor may the elders [always] understand justice" **(Job 32:9 AMP).**

Those who have had experience have gained some knowledge. You can buy a walking stick, but gray hair comes with age. *"Is not wisdom found among the aged? Does not long-life bring understanding?"* (Job 12:12 NIV). As much as it is a good practice to seek the counsel of others, it is not compulsory, however, to take to any advice that

> THOSE WHO HAVE HAD EXPERIENCE HAVE GAINED SOME KNOWLEDGE. YOU CAN BUY A WALKING STICK, BUT GRAY HAIR COMES WITH AGE

is against good judgement, unkind, immoral or fruitless. The advantage of wisdom is discernment and discernment help to differentiate truth from error and right from wrong.

"12 So Jeroboam and all the people came to Rehoboam the third day, as the king had directed, saying, "Come back to me the third day." 13 Then the king answered the people roughly, and rejected the advice which the elders had given him; 14 and he spoke to them according to the advice of the young men, saying, "My father made your yoke heavy, but I will add to your yoke; my father chastised you with whips, but I will chastise you with scourges!" 15 So the king did not listen to the people; for the turn of events was from the Lord, that He might fulfill His word, which

the Lord had spoken by Ahijah the Shilonite to Jeroboam the son of Nebat" **(2 Chronicles 10:12-15).**

Recklessness Is a Sign of Immaturity

The young king did not heed the counsel of the elders to speak kindly to his people, instead he took to the advice of the young men (his peers) and spoke roughly to the people. The king failed to communicate to the people how important and vital they were to him and to the kingdom. He underestimated the impact that kind words or kindness can have on people,

> AS MUCH AS IT IS A GOOD PRACTICE TO SEEK THE COUNSEL OF OTHERS, IT IS NOT COMPULSORY, HOWEVER TO TAKE TO ANY ADVICE THAT IS AGAINST GOOD JUDGEMENT, UNKIND, IMMORAL OR FRUITLESS

and in this case, it could have won the people over. Kind words of affirmation make people feel valued and people want to be around people who make them feel important.

The king's words were graceless like that of a despotic tyrant and his unkindness incited the people to rebellion against himself; he lost their loyalty, and the kingdom of Israel was divided into two unequal parts from this point onwards.

> *"16 Now when all Israel saw that the king did not listen to them, the people answered the king, saying: "What share have we in David? We have no inheritance in the son of Jesse. Every man to your tents, O Israel! Now see to your own house, O David!" So, Israel departed to their tents. 17 But Rehoboam reigned over the children of Israel who dwelt in the cities of Judah"* **(2 Chronicles 10:16-17).**

Here is an instance of a prince who lost everything because of foolish pride and unkind words. He was aware of the problems that existed prior to him being king and could have been wiser in his actions and because he rejected wisdom, he paid dearly for it and set his descendants up for perpetual rifts and generational conflicts with the other tribes. Lack of wisdom is responsible for reckless behavior in many youths. The king failed to realize that the crown was at stake and that it is the people who keep the crown on the head of their king and for the sake of the crown, a little compromise would have done no harm. Wisdom suggests at a time like this for concession rather than coercion, for compromise rather than compulsion, because it was evident that rebellion was in the air.

> KIND WORDS OF AFFIRMATION MAKE PEOPLE FEEL VALUED AND PEOPLE WANT TO BE AROUND PEOPLE WHO MAKE THEM FEEL IMPORTANT

History is replete with stories and examples of good fathers with bad children, wise fathers and foolish children and of course sometimes, bad fathers who had good children. Rehoboam was the son of king Solomon, the man considered to be the wisest man who ever lived, and you would think Rehoboam would have shown a little of his father's wisdom. It is sad to know that Rehoboam, like many others, do not make good of their special privileges.

> WISDOM SUGGESTS AT A TIME LIKE THIS FOR CONCESSION RATHER THAN COERCION, FOR COMPROMISE RATHER THAN COMPULSION, BECAUSE IT WAS EVIDENT THAT REBELLION WAS IN THE AIR

Had the king been asked to pay tons of gold or silver to keep his kingdom, would he not have paid it and expended himself? But he failed to pay something as costless as kind words and because of his recklessness, he paid the price of separating his family from the rest of Israel and undid in a moment the legacy of a century old dynasty.

Winning with Kind Words

CHAPTER 3

"The tongue of the wise uses knowledge rightly, but the mouth of fools pours forth foolishness "
(Proverbs 15:2).

Joseph, Boaz, Ruth, David, Abigail, and Paul the Apostle all have one thing in common; they knew the secret of winning with kind words.

> *"He who would love life and see good days, let him refrain his tongue from evil, and his lips from speaking deceit"* **(1 Peter 3:10).**

Joseph

After the death of Jacob, the sons of Jacob were afraid that their brother Joseph, the Prime Minister of Egypt might now retaliate for all the evil they had done to him. They came to him in great fear and in total surrender, bowed before him and said, *"We are your servants,"* thereby fulfilling the prophetic dream Joseph had while he was a young man.

> *"18 Then his brothers themselves came and bowed down before him. "Here we are before you as your slaves," they said. 19 But Joseph said to them, **"Don't be afraid; I can't put myself in the place of God. 20 You plotted evil against me, but God turned it into good,** in order to preserve the lives of many people who are alive today because of what happened. 21 You have nothing to fear. I will take care of you and your children." So, he reassured them with kind words that touched their hearts"* **(Genesis 50:18-21 GNT).**

Joseph, knowing their fears, spoke kindly to them and reassured them with comforting words. Joseph was able to mend the many years of broken relationship with his family and relieved his brothers of their guilt and fears. Kind words may win your adversary rather than vengeful words.

The Winning Way

Though Joseph was in a place to avenge himself and mete out justice to his brothers and allow them a taste of their own bitter medicine. Joseph chose a more noble way; "The Way of Forgiveness." Some say, *"Vengeance is sweet,"* but the truth is revenge is rarely sweet. It might give the avenger a temporary feeling of satisfaction, but the feeling soon turns into dissatisfaction. Francis Bacon, an English Stateman, once said, *"In taking revenge, a man is but even with his enemy; but in passing it over, he is superior."*

> IN TAKING REVENGE, A MAN IS BUT EVEN WITH HIS ENEMY; BUT IN PASSING IT OVER, HE IS SUPERIOR

How Joseph Was Able to Forgive

Personal hardships have a way of making us human and tender towards others. It is easy to judge and be critical of people who have the kinds of problems we are unaccustomed to. It is evident that Joseph's **personal faith** in God is key to understanding his readiness to forgive his brothers. Forgiveness does not come easily except by enabling grace.

Also, Joseph had an **unwavering faith in God's plan for his life,** though his life took many odd turns at times, he believed that God had a plan and a purpose for his life and was convinced that His promise (the dream) to him will not fail. The strength of divine purpose is that it still makes rough roads lead to the right places.

We spend a significant amount of time in the "in-between" places before destiny. The in-between place of life is a temporary holding place, where God prepares us for where we are going next. For Moses it was the wilderness of Midian, for Israel it was the wilderness, and for David it was the years as a shepherd on the field and the many years as an anointed wanderer.

> THE STRENGTH OF DIVINE PURPOSE IS THAT IT STILL MAKES ROUGH ROADS LEAD TO THE RIGHT PLACES

Sadly, it is in this place many trade their life's purpose; they get distracted, fail to learn the lesson they need to move on and therefore disqualify themselves for their promotion or next place. For Joseph it was Egypt, then Potiphar's house and next in the prison. So, while Joseph awaits his dream to come to pass, God was also preparing him for where he was going, to the top. Joseph soon realized that there were few things he needed to deal with if his dreams were to come true. First, was the pain from his past which was caused by his family, and second, was the challenge of forgiving his brothers. It was evident to him that unless he dealt with these issues, he could not

> MANY GLORIOUS DREAMS ARE HELD UP BECAUSE MANY ARE STILL COURTING THE DEMONS OF PAST PAINS AND ALLOWING THEMSELVES TO BE PRISONERS OF UNFORGIVENESS

make any progress. Many glorious dreams are held up because many are still courting the demons of past pains and allowing themselves to be prisoners of unforgiveness.

Healing Is Not Possible Without Forgiveness

Joseph never knew much of family love, for his family had betrayed him when he was just a young child. In Egypt Joseph found a new family of his own, a loving wife and children which gave him the much-needed family support and a meaningful relationship he had missed all these years. The names he gave to his children gives us insight to what had transpired in his personal life and the progress he had made in the journey to healing.

> *"⁵⁰And to Joseph were born two sons* before the years of famine came, whom Asenath, the daughter of Poti-Pherah priest of On, bore to him. *⁵¹Joseph called the name of the firstborn Manasseh: "For God has made me forget all my toil and all my father's house"* **(Genesis 41:50-51).**

Healing Is in Stages

Joseph named his firstborn Manasseh, meaning *"God has made me forget all my trouble and hardship and all [the sorrow of the loss of] my father's household"* (Genesis 41:51 AMP). In other words, God helped him to heal from the wounds of his past. He did not say, "God made me to discount the pain of my past," but rather forget it. If you can forget, then you can forgive. Joseph was able to **deal with his past troubles and his injurers,** and put it all in the past

AS A CANOE CANNOT MOVE FORWARD UNTIL IT IS FIRST ROWED BACKWARD, YOU ALSO CANNOT MOVE FORWARD UNTIL YOU BRING BACK THE PAINFUL ISSUES OF THE PAST AND DEAL WITH THEM IN THE PRESENT once and for all with by God's help. As a canoe cannot move forward until it is first rowed backward, you also cannot move forward until you bring back the painful issues of the past and deal with them in the present.

To heal from your wounds, you will need to bring forward the pain, deal with it by admitting whatever it was, and submit your story to God, and then release your injurers, that is, forgive those who hurt you. By doing so you also release yourself from them, leaving them all in your past. If you have in your hand a rope tied to a moving train, what is the sure thing to do to prevent the train from dragging you to your death? Is it not to *"Let go?"* Yes, Let Go!

> UNFORGIVENESS IS LIKE DRINKING POISON AND EXPECTING SOMEONE ELSE TO DIE FROM IT

Forgiveness, in reality is not what we do for others but what we do for ourselves. It is more than doing your injurers a favor, but the first benefit is that it helps you detach from the hold the whole experience has had on you. It removes malice and resentments from your heart and begins the healing process.

Someone said, *"unforgiveness is like drinking poison and expecting someone else to die from it."* It is also like serving jail time for somebody else's crime. After forgiving them, then declare that you are leaving them all in the past. Lose the pain but not the lesson.

*"And the name of the second **he called Ephraim: 'For God has caused me to be fruitful in the land of my affliction"** (Genesis 41:52).*

Joseph named his second-born Ephraim, meaning *"God has caused me to be fruitful in the land of my affliction."* After Joseph had dealt with the pain of his past, he now **affirms and acknowledges the present.** To affirm the present is to understand the "Power of Now," to acknowledge the good things happening now. Reliving the pain of the

> **RELIVING THE PAIN OF THE PAST ROBS YOU FROM ENJOYING THE BLESSINGS OF THE PRESENT**

past robs you from enjoying the blessings of the present. Look around; something good is happening. God will see to it that something good comes out of your bad experiences.

> *"And we know that all things work together for good to those who love God, to those who are the called according to His purpose"* **(Romans 8:28).**

If you look carefully in your own story, there is at least one thing you can thank God for because God will never leave you without something to thank Him for. When

> **IF YOU LOOK CAREFULLY IN YOUR OWN STORY, THERE IS ONE THING YOU CAN THANK GOD FOR**

Joseph looked back on his life and mulled over his own story, even though he had a painful beginning, and travelled long on many rough roads, it was this same path that brought him to the place where his dreams come true, though his brothers regretted their actions and were sorry for the mistreatments of their little brother, Joseph accepted and realized the truth that all of this had to have happened, for him to reach the position of becoming Egypt's prime minister.

Joseph's brothers were not the only one who mistreated him: Potiphar's wife, his master's mistress lied on him, and he ended up in jail, none of his colleagues who knew him well spoke out to defend his character, and the king's butler forgot to remember Joseph's kindness on time. It appeared as if dreams could not come true in a prison, but the prison can be a pre-season of life. There have been many who like Joseph that came out of prisons to become presidents of their nations i.e., (Nelson Mandela, Oluwasegun Obasanjo, Jawaharlal Nehru, Aung San Suu Kyi, Vaclav Havel, Michelle Bache). Sometimes dreams may die before they live again.

It is a pattern with God to repay evil with good and to give victory on the same ground one was once defeated and turn hard trials to great testimonies.

> IT IS A PATTERN WITH GOD TO REPAY EVIL WITH GOD AND TO GIVE VICTORY ON THE SAME GROUND ONE WAS ONCE DEFEATED AND TURN HARD TRIALS TO GREAT TESTIMONIES

Joseph was able to forgive his brothers because he allowed God to work in and through him, and because he forgave his brothers, he brought his family back together and secured a prominent and prosperous future for his own descendants among the tribes of Israel.

> "No temptation has overtaken you except such as is common to man; **but God is faithful, who will not allow you to be tempted beyond what you are able, but with the temptation will also make the way of escape,** that you may be able to bear it" **(1 Corinthians 10:13).**

How Joseph Healed and Was Able to Forgive

- Joseph had a **personal faith** in God.
- Joseph **maintained an unwavering faith in God's plan for his life.**
- Joseph was willing to **deal with his past troubles (wounds) and forgive his injurers.**
- Joseph did not fail to **affirm and acknowledge the present.**
- Joseph realized and **accepted the truth that all of this had to happen for his dreams to come true.**

Boaz and Ruth

Ruth's story provides us lessons in love, faith, favor, discipline, courage, diligence and purpose. Ruth takes the central place in the book named after her. However, it is difficult to ignore the other characters mentioned in the story from whom we also learn practical and helpful life lessons.

The story of Boaz and Ruth is very appealing; nowhere else in the Scriptures is true love and romance vividly portrayed than here. Other than in fairy tales, this kind of love story is very hard to come by. And unlike some have suggested, Ruth didn't initiate the love relationship between her and Boaz. It was in fact Boaz that sparked her interest, she only responded to Boaz's unexpected kindness towards her.

> *"⁸Then Boaz said to Ruth, 'You will listen, my daughter, will you not? Do not go to glean in another field, nor go from here, but stay close by my young women. ⁹ Let your eyes be on the field which they reap and go after them. Have I not commanded the young men not to touch you? And when you are thirsty, go to the vessels and drink from what the young men have drawn'"* (Ruth 2:8-9).

It was this interest and special favor from Boaz that won a bride for him. It is true that kind deeds or kind words are like seeds, once sown will bring harvest. Anyone who must have friends must first be friendly. Boaz won Ruth's affection by his kind words.

> *"Then she said, 'I have found favor in your sight, my lord, for you have comforted me and indeed have spoken kindly to your maidservant though I am not like one of your maidservants'"* (Ruth 2:13 NASB).

Nabal: The Portrait of a Fool

The name Nabal means foolish or senseless, he was a descendant of Caleb from Maon in the highlands of Judah, about seven miles south-east of Hebron. Nabal was a sheep master and had become very wealthy because of his thousands of sheep and goats.

> *"²Now there was a man in Maon whose business was in Carmel, and the man was very rich. He had three thousand sheep and a thousand goats. And he was shearing his sheep in Carmel. ³The name of the man was Nabal, and the name of his wife Abigail. And she was a*

woman of good understanding and beautiful appearance; **but the man was harsh and evil in his doings.** *He was of the house of Caleb.* *4When David heard in the wilderness that Nabal was shearing his sheep"* **(1 Samuel 25:2-4).**

David had been traveling and camping in the wilderness and at a point in time met with Nabal's shepherds. David and his men were unusually kind to Nabals shepherds; they protected them day and night from desert raiders. The nomadic life is not only challenging but dangerous; it is a constant vigil between evil beasts and evil men. Armed men or raiders would often prance on shepherds to kill them for their flocks and supplies.

Though David was not yet king, he was just as famous in the land as the king himself. He was a warrior and if he wanted anything he could get it either by request or by force, but David was a godly man, he was a just man and a great example for his followers. When David ran low on provisions for his men, he sent word to Nabal asking him for provisions for his men in hope that Nabal would remember his kindness to his men and flocks while they were with him in Carmel.

"5And David sent ten young men, and said to them, go up to Carmel and **go to Nabal, and say kind words to him in my name;** *...... 14But one of the young men said to Nabal's wife Abigail, David sent men from the waste land to say kind words to our master,* **and he gave them a rough answer"** **(1 Samuel 25:5,14 BBE-Bible in Basic English).**

Nabal's Angry Denial

Unfortunately, Nabal didn't have kind words for David, his response was not only surprising but his words and insult to David were unwarranted. You must be an ingrate to forget kindness towards you and a fool to provoke the wrath of an armed man. His unbridled tongue almost cost him the life of every male in his household, if not for the intervention of Abigail his wife who **saved the day by her wisdom and kind words** to David.

> "10*Then Nabal answered David's servants, and said,* **"Who is David, and who is the son of Jesse?** *There are many servants nowadays who break away each one from his master.* **11Shall I then take my bread and my water** *and my meat that I have killed for my shearers,* **and give it to men when I do not know where they are from?"** 12*So David's young men turned on their heels and went back; and they came and told him all these words"* **(1 Samuel 25:10-12).**

> *"A fool speaks foolishly and thinks up evil things to do.* **What he does and what he says are an insult to the Lord, and he never feeds the hungry or gives thirsty people anything to drink"** **(Isaiah 32:6 GNT-Good News Translation).**

Nabal had only one thing going for him, a beautiful and wise wife. Although he was a rich man, he was considered a fool. Nabal died ten days after speaking so carelessly to David, it is unwise to despise the anointed of the Lord. On this point A. B. Simpson wrote, *"I'd rather play with lightning than speak a reckless word against a servant of Christ."*

"Whoever guards his mouth and tongue keeps his soul from troubles" **(Proverbs 21:23).**

Charles Haddon Spurgeon remarked that, "Wisdom is the right use of knowledge. To know is not to be wise. Many men know a great deal and are all the greater fools for it. There is no fool so great a fool as a knowing fool. But to know how to use knowledge is to have wisdom."

A Crisis Was Unavoidable

"A hot-tempered man stirs up strife, but the slow to anger calms a dispute" **(Proverbs 15:18 NASB).**

"Who is David and who is the son of Jesse?" These were Nabal's mocking questions; they were meant to insult David and debase his family. David was very popular throughout the land; everyone knew who David was. His heroic act of saving the nation from the Philistines and killing Goliath (the giant from Gath) had etched him in the minds of the people as their hero. And it is unlikely that Nabal was unaware of who David was because he did call him by his father's name, *"Who is David and who is the son of Jesse?"* Nabal was just being sarcastic and in his contempt refused to acknowledge David's past achievements (killing Goliath) nor his future as king.

Nabal thought himself as the rich and successful tycoon from Carmel, and David and his men as outlaws and rebels. And he had no time for rag-tags, gypsies and beggars. He angrily denied David's request and as a result David became enraged by Nabal's insult and insensitivity.

"13 Then David said to his men, 'Every man gird on his sword.' So, every man girded on his sword, and David also girded on his sword. And about four hundred men went with David, and two hundred stayed with the supplies. 14 Now one of the young men told Abigail, Nabal's wife, saying, 'Look, David sent messengers from the wilderness to greet our master; and he reviled them. 15 But the men were very good to us, and we were not hurt, nor did we miss anything as long as we accompanied them, when we were in the fields. 16 They were a wall to us both by night and day, all the time we were with them keeping the sheep. 17 Now therefore, know and consider what you will do, for harm is determined against our master and against all his household. For he is such a scoundrel that one cannot speak to him'"*

(1 Samuel 25:13-17).

Abigail

It was this crisis that introduced us to Abigail, the woman who found herself between two angry men. Abigail's quick decision, wisdom, courage and negotiating skills are highly commendable and a formula for crisis intervention. She leaves a legacy on how-to examples for women who have married fools and or are in abusive relationships.

*"2Now there was a man in Maon whose business was in Carmel, and the man was very rich. He had three thousand sheep and a thousand goats. And he was shearing his sheep in Carmel. 3The name of the man was Nabal, and **the name of his wife Abigail. And she was a woman of good understanding and beautiful***

appearance; but the man was harsh and evil in his doings. He was of the house of Caleb" **(1 Samuel 25:2-3).**

Notice how Abigail was first described, by her quality characters, unlike her husband who was first described by his possessions and then his lousy character. Nabal was harsh and evil in his dealings; he was insensitive and a graceless businessman.

Abigail was a woman of great beauty and compelling wisdom. Beautiful women with good character and wisdom are gems, very rare; and it is both a marvel and unfortunate how oftentimes these women end up with Nabals (fools). Abigail has been able to survive her abusive husband and sustain her marriage to Nabal by her godly wisdom. Solomon the king writes,

> BEAUTIFUL WOMEN WITH GOOD CHARACTER AND WISDOM ARE GEMS, VERY RARE; AND IT IS BOTH A MARVEL AND UNFORTUNATE HOW OFTENTIMES THESE WOMEN END UP WITH NABALS (FOOLS)

> *"**The wise woman builds her house,** but the foolish pulls it down with her hands"* **(Proverbs 14:1)**.

How Abigail Disarmed a Captain and Four Hundred Fighting Soldiers

No one would have believed that a simple unarmed woman could have managed to disarm a notable fighter and his four hundred fighting soldiers but surprisingly, this woman accomplished such a feat. Her godly wisdom and bravery, won and saved the day for her household.

There is no problem, no matter how difficult that wisdom cannot solve. Most of what we call problems are only wisdom deficit problems, in other words you don't have a financial problem or a marital problem you only have a wisdom problem and problems only last as long as you are able to gain a new perspective on how to solve them. You cannot solve your problems on the same level you created it. Problems entwines, but wisdom unravels. Abigail's actions were guided by wisdom and the outcome of wisdom is success.

> PROBLEMS ONLY LAST AS LONG AS YOU ARE ABLE TO GAIN A NEW PERSPECTIVE ON HOW TO SOLVE THEM. PROBLEMS ENTWINES, BUT WISDOM UNRAVELS

> *"If the axe is dull and he does not sharpen its edge, then he must exert more strength. **Wisdom has the advantage of giving success**" (Ecclesiastes 10:10 NASB).*

> **"Wisdom is the principal thing; therefore, get wisdom.** *And in all your getting, **get understanding**"* (Proverbs 4:7).

The Wisdom of Promptness

Abigail needed to act promptly. The crisis demands quick decisive action for there were many lives at stake. She knew there was no use deliberating with her unreasonable husband, she must get to David before it was too late.

> *"18**Then Abigail hurried** and took two hundred loaves of bread and two jugs of wine and five sheep already prepared and five measures of roasted grain and a hundred clusters*

of raisins and two hundred cakes of figs and loaded them on donkeys. 19 And she said to her servants, 'Go on before me; see, I am coming after you.' But she did not tell her husband Nabal" **(1 Samuel 25:18-19).**

Thrice the Bible noted, *"She made haste"* (1 Samuel 25:18, 23, 42). Promptness is a habit of wise and successful people. When opportunities are met by promptness the result is success. There are many who have missed golden opportunities because of

> IT IS UNAVAILING TO DO THE RIGHT THING AT THE WRONG TIME

untimeliness. It is unavailing to do the right thing at the wrong time. Lord Chesterfield, British Statesman and man of letters said, *"Promptness is the soul of business."*

> *"20 So it was, as she rode on the donkey, that she went down under cover of the hill; and there were David and his men, coming down toward her, and she met them. 21 Now David had said, 'Surely in vain I have protected all that this fellow has in the wilderness, so that nothing was missed of all that belongs to him. And he has repaid me evil for good. 22 May God do so, and more also, to the enemies of David, if I leave one male of all who belong to him by morning light.' 23 Now when Abigail saw David, she dismounted quickly from the donkey, fell on her face before David, and bowed down to the ground. 24 So she fell at his feet and said: 'On me, my lord, on me let this iniquity be! And please let your maidservant speak in your ears, and hear the words of your maidservant'"* **(1 Samuel 25:20-24).**

The Wisdom of Strategic Planning

"The plans of the diligent lead surely to advantage ..." (Proverbs 21:5a NASB).

Abigail had a very careful and well-thought-out strategy on how to manage the crisis at hand. She had experience in managing situations; the princess has survived living with a thug. This beauty is married to the beast, and now she's caught between two angry men; she will need her wits again on how to manage the situation. She knows quite well that

> WHEN TWO ELEPHANTS FIGHT, IT'S THE GRASS THAT SUFFEROS

when two elephants fight, it's the grass that suffers and when two fools fight only the innocent suffers. Her plan is a classic method in crisis intervention. Jesus teaching about planning said,

> "Or what king, when he sets out to meet another king in battle, will not **first sit down and consider** whether he is strong enough with ten thousand men to encounter the one coming against him with twenty thousand?" **(Luke 14:31 NASB).**

She sent an envoy ahead. She did not tell her undiscerning husband. She was familiar with the countryside, and she went down under cover of the hills. She was in a vantage position where she could see David first. She took David off guard with her humility, beauty and wisdom.

> **"Plans are established by counsel; so, make war [only] with wise guidance"** **(Proverbs 20:18 AMP).**

> **"²³Now when Abigail saw David, she dismounted quickly from the donkey, fell on her face before David, and bowed down to the ground. ²⁴So she fell at his feet** and said: 'On me, my lord, on me let this iniquity be! And please let your maidservant speak in your ears and hear the words of your maidservant.

25Please, let not my lord regard this scoundrel Nabal. For as his name is, so is he: Nabal is his name, and folly is with him! But I, your maidservant, did not see the young men of my lord whom you sent'" **(1 Samuel 25:23-25).**

The Wisdom of Humility

Humility and kindness are conjoined traits of a great personality; kind words are the wise man's choice. It is easier to be proud than humble. Abigail approached David with such great humility; her physical pose conveyed her message. Her every movement was downward. *"She went down under cover of the hill,"* when she saw David, *"she dismounted from her donkey,"* *"fell before David's face on her face,"* *"bowed toward the ground at his feet."* Such a display of humility is not only noticeable but captivating.

> HUMILITY AND KINDNESS ARE CONJOINED TRAITS OF A GREAT PERSONALITY; KIND WORDS ARE THE WISE MAN'S CHOICE.

In the ten verses that describes her encounter with David, we noted she addressed David as *"my lord"* eight times and herself as *"your maidservant"* six different times. Her words and actions show complete surrender; she does not accuse David of anything nor dismiss his anger, but wisely appealed to David's godliness.

*"When pride comes, then comes shame; **but with the humble is wisdom"*** **(Proverbs 11:2).**

The Effect of Humility

Some men can be unreasonable and difficult to deal with, but this is true with most men, that a non-threatening and humble approach by a woman will win most of the time. Women in relationships should apply this principle of wisdom through humility; it has proven to be a winning method. Maybe the best way to deal with a man is to make him feel he doesn't need to put up his guard. Any confrontation naturally turns on his defenses and makes him put up his guard. The old wise king is still right after 3,000 years:

> A NON-THREATENING AND HUMBLE APPROACH BY A WOMAN WILL WIN MOST OF THE TIME

"A soft answer turns away wrath" (Proverbs 15:1a).

Abigail's humility and kind words won her the right to appeal for mercy and reconsideration from David. Nabal was the object of David's anger and his anger was to be carried out when he finds him. David was unprepared for Abigail's interception. She ambushed David by sending the provisions ahead of her, and now she is at his feet in total surrender saying,

"My lord, I am the one you are looking for, am the one at fault, and on me you should take out your anger, if you please" (paraphrased).

David was not looking to fight or kill a woman especially one like this who is so prudent, humble, and strikingly beautiful. David was completely taken off guard by Abigail's humbleness. Even though Abigail is bowed before David she was nevertheless in control of the whole situation. She had proven the wisdom of humility and showed that truly humility is strength. To possess beauty, wisdom and humility is certainly a winning combination. Alexander Maclaren sums it up in this statement, *"Kindness makes a person attractive. If you would win the world, melt it, do not hammer it."*

> KINDNESS MAKES A PERSON ATTRACTIVE. IF YOU WOULD WIN THE WORLD, MELT IT DO NOT HAMMER IT

Anger is Just One Letter Short of Danger

How do you approach an angry man, an armed angry man for that matter? I guess you do the same way you approach an explosive device, with great caution. Explosive specialists know how to handle explosives and time-bombs; they know not to rough handle or aggravate the device; this is not a job for novices. To negotiate a very tense and dangerous situation requires great skill, negotiators and explosive specialists have the patience and the wisdom to defuse threatening situations. Abigail's kind words diffused David's anger thereby averting the disaster planned against her household. Abigail's appeal to David was to disregard her foolish

> TO NEGOTIATE A VERY TENSE AND DANGEROUS SITUATION REQUIRES GREAT SKILL

56

husband and to rid himself of his anger and the impulsive oath to kill all male persons of Nabal's household. She addressed David as her lord while she called her own husband *"this scoundrel."* These were not flattering words but kind and peaceful words to an angry man in the hope that he might reconsider his position.

> *"If you are sensible, you will control your temper. When someone wrongs you, it is a great virtue to ignore it"* **(Proverbs 19:11 GNT).**

Abigail's point is; my husband Nabal isn't worth your time and you wouldn't achieve much dealing with a fool. The old wise king writes, *"Though you grind a fool in a mortar with a pestle along with crushed grain, yet his foolishness will not depart from him"* **(Proverbs 27:22).** Therefore, to respond to Nabal would be acting like him, *"Do not answer a fool according to his folly, lest you also be like him"* **(Proverbs 26:4).**

The Wisdom of Godly Counsel

> *"Charm is deceitful, and beauty is passing, but a woman who fears the LORD, she shall be praised"* **(Proverbs 31:30).**

Though Abigail was wise and beautiful, her greatest quality was her faith in the God of Israel. She redirected David's attention from the foolish pursuit of Nabal, to the focus on God's plan for his future, which Abigail proved to be very much familiar with. Abigail's knowledge of God and strong faith in God had birthed within her a strong hope for the future of the nation which she believed David was key.

> *"26 Now therefore, my lord, as the Lord lives and as your soul lives, since the Lord has held you back from coming to bloodshed and from avenging yourself with your own hand, now then, let your enemies and those who seek harm for my lord be as Nabal. 27 And now this present which your maidservant has brought to my lord, let it be given to the young men who follow my lord. 28 Please forgive the trespass of your maidservant. For the Lord will certainly make for my lord an enduring house, because my lord fights the battles of the Lord, and evil is not found in you throughout your days. 29 Yet a man has risen to pursue you and seek your life, but the life of my lord shall be bound in the bundle of the living with the Lord your God; and the lives of your enemies He shall sling out, as from the pocket of a sling. 30And when the Lord has done for my lord all those good things which he has said he will do for you, and has made you a ruler over Israel; 31Then you will have no cause for grief, and my lord's heart will not be troubled because you have taken life without cause and have yourself given punishment for your wrongs: and when the Lord has been good to you, then give a thought to your servant"* **(1 Samuel 25:26-31).**

The Power of Biblical Counsel

*"Where there is no counsel, the people fall; but **in the multitude of counselors there is safety"** **(Proverbs 11:14).**

Abigail asked for permission to speak to David and once granted, she humbly advised David in such detailed manner. In 1 Samuel 25, notice how she began, "Let your maidservant speak" vs. 24, "Let not my lord regard this scoundrel" vs. 25, "Let the Lord avenge you" vs. 26, "Let all your enemies be as fools" vs. 26, "Let the provisions be given to the men" vs. 27, "Please forgive your maidservant" vs. 28, "The Lord has determined to reward and establish you" vs. 28, "The Lord will protect and preserve you for his purpose" vs. 29, "The Lord will fulfill his promise to you concerning the throne of Israel" vs. 30, and "Please remember your maidservant when the Lord fulfill his promise to David" vs. 31.

This rare faith is what had a tremendous impact on David more than her wisdom and beauty. David had shown he could wait for God's time, but the day to day hunt and endless pursuit for his life had made waiting a burden.

Abigail reassured David of God's promises and purpose for his life also advised David to allow God to avenge him rather than avenging himself and be guilty of mass murder.

She was also aware of the many murderous attempts of King Saul on David's life, so she humbly argued, what difference would there be between King Saul and David, if David proceeded to shed innocent blood? Benjamin Franklin once said, *"He that won't be counseled, cannot be helped."*

> HE THAT WON'T BE COUNSELED, CANNOT BE HELPED

David is now made to think on these things, and with his anger now defused, he gained a new perspective on the situation at hand.

One of the effective methods of dealing with anger is to distract yourself, that is, to turn your attention elsewhere. In this case, Abigail was the distraction for David's anger.

Let's not dismiss or disregard those whom God sends our way with instructions for our lives; disregarding them could cost us dearly.

> *"The way of a fool is right in his own eyes, **but he who heeds counsel is wise"* (Proverbs 12:15)*.

The Advantage of Familiarity with God's Plan

Abigail greatest persuasion comes from her familiarity with David's prophetic future, and therefore, was able to help him focus on His destiny. It is unwise to give up a glorious future for a moment of relieving anger or satisfying revenge.

IT IS UNWISE TO GIVE UP A GLORIOUS FUTURE FOR A MOMENT OF RELIEVING ANGER OR SATISFYING REVENGE.

Abigail reminded David that God had promised to make him king of Israel with the blessing of an endless dynasty.

It is also true that God has made many precious promises in the Holy Scriptures to every believer. Therefore, the Christian is to live carefully and in concert with the Word of God for the realization of destiny.

> *"Therefore, brethren, **be even more diligent to make your call and election sure,** for if you do these things, you will never stumble"* (2 Peter 1:10)*.

Discovering God's will is like having the manual or the blueprint for life. A manual supplies instruction and outlines the design of a product, be it as handy as a camera or as complex as a car. A manual is a blueprint. When we know God's plan for our lives, we can live life by design instead of by default. As we see life through the lens of heaven, and daily align our thoughts and actions in the light of God's plans, the result is peace, love, joy, satisfaction and happiness.

> WHEN WE KNOW GOD'S PLAN FOR OUR LIVES, WE CAN LIVE LIFE BY DESIGN INSTEAD OF BY DEFAULT. AS WE SEE LIFE THROUGH THE LENS OF HEAVEN, AND DAILY ALIGN OUR THOUGHTS AND ACTIONS IN THE LIGHT OF GOD'S PLANS, THE RESULT IS PEACE, LOVE, JOY, SATISFACTION AND HAPPINESS.

Also, the advantage of familiarity with God's plan is self-knowledge; the belief in one-self and the purpose of God in one's life. Jesus was full of self-knowledge, He knew His purpose and more importantly, He knew who He was.

He was always declaring who He was; *"I am the Way, the Truth, and the Life"*. *"I am the Good Shepherd"* ... *"I am the Door."* When the Devil questioned Jesus' identity and asked Him to prove if He were the Son of God (Matthew 4:4). Jesus simply ignored him and didn't have to prove Himself, because He was sure who He was and knew also that the Devil knew who He was. Jesus found his life's purpose as He searched the Scriptures.

> THE ADVANTAGE OF FAMILIARITY WITH GOD'S PLAN IS SELF-KNOWLEDGE; THE BELIEF IN ONE-SELF AND THE PURPOSE OF GOD IN ONE'S LIFE

Furthermore, Jesus was not afraid to face His enemies even death, because he knew the plan of God for Him; He knew His life's purpose. While in Pilate's court, Pilate taunted Him with the idea that he had the power to crucify or release Him, but Jesus told Pilate that he could not do more than God allowed him in the matter. Another advantage of familiarity with God's plan is confident living.

> "So, Pilate asked him, 'Are you a king, then? Jesus answered, 'You say that I am a king'. **I was born and came into the world for this one purpose,** to speak about the truth. Whoever belongs to the truth listens to me." **(John 18:37 GNT).**

> "Pilate said to him, 'You will not speak to me? Remember, **I have the authority to set you free and also to have you crucified.' Jesus answered, 'You have authority over me only because it was given to you by God.** So, the man who handed me over to you is guilty of a worse sin." **(John 19:10-11 GNT).**

Jesus was bold to say to the religious leaders and the crowd that He came to fulfill the law (that which was written concerning Him).

> **"Behold, I come; in the scroll of the book, it is written of me. I delight to do Your will,** O my God, and Your law is within my heart" **(Psalm 40:7-8).**

He found His life's purpose as He searched the Scriptures. You will find God's purpose for your life also if you will prayerfully search and look for it in God's Word, because Jesus was familiar with God's plan for His life, He was able to live every day fulfilling that purpose.

> *"16So He came to Nazareth, where He had been brought up. **And as His custom was, He went into the synagogue on the Sabbath day, and stood up to read.** 17 And He was handed the book of the prophet Isaiah. **And when He had opened the book, He found the place where it was written:** 18'The Spirit of the Lord is upon Me, because He has anointed Me to preach the gospel to the poor; He has sent Me to heal the brokenhearted, to proclaim liberty to the captives and recovery of sight to the blind, to set at liberty those who are oppressed; 19to proclaim the acceptable year of the Lord.' 20Then He closed the book, and gave it back to the attendant and sat down. And the eyes of all who were in the synagogue were fixed on Him 21And He began to say to them, 'Today this Scripture is fulfilled in your hearing'" (Luke 4:16-21).*

The first step in knowing God's will for your life is by prayer, certainly the most obvious answer to the question of *'how do I know God's will for my life'*? is asking Him directly.

> *'I cry out to God Most High, to God who will fulfill His purpose for me'.* **(Psalm 52:7 NLT).**

God's primary way of speaking to us is through the Bible, so studying the Bible will help us discover and confirm God's purpose for our lives. Now, you won't find any verses that will tell you to become a social worker, or a teacher, but you will discover what you need to do when you understand the heart of God.

The Negative Impact
Of Undermining Words

CHAPTER 4

---

*"If you would derail a man's purpose,
you may not fight him with swords
and spears, but you could affect his resolve
with unkind and fear-provoking words."*
-Bishop Michael Atunrase

THE NATURE OF WORDS is that it is both invasive and pervasive; words do affect every area of the personality. Our words can regulate or determine other people's responses. Your words can change how people feel about themselves, and how they feel about their lives or their work.

> YOUR WORDS CAN CHANGE HOW PEOPLE FEEL ABOUT THEMSELVES, AND HOW THEY FEEL ABOUT THEIR LIVES OR THEIR WORK

Under the leadership of Nehemiah, the Children of Israel decided to rebuild the walls of Jerusalem that had broken down for many years, but their enemies (Sanballat and his co-conspirators) fiercely opposed them.

Sanballat's purpose was to discourage the Jews so that they would abandon their God given task. He launched a series of attacks to stop them from rebuilding the wall. His foremost strategy was the use of undermining and fear-inducing words to demoralize the people because he knew if he could dampen their spirits; he could abort their mission.

Kind and uplifting words can encourage people to pursue their mission, while negative and uninspiring words create self-doubt and can cause people to lose courage and give up their mission.

> NEGATIVE WORDS TURN INTO NEGATIVE BELIEFS

Negative words turn into negative beliefs. If you would derail a man's purpose, you may not fight him with swords and spears, but you could affect his resolve with unkind and fear-provoking words.

"For they all wanted to frighten us, thinking, "They will become discouraged with the work and it will not be done." But now, [O God,] strengthen my hands" **(Nehemiah 6:9 AMP).**

Unkind Words as a Tool of the Enemy to Distract and Derail Purpose

The Bible says, *"Faith comes by hearing"* (Romans 10:17). Our actions, whether good or bad, are determined by our 'hearing' (what we hear). There is a connection between what *we hear* and what *we do*. There are two major canals in the human body, the ear canal and the birth canal. One is a gateway in and the other is a gateway out. It stands to reason then, that whatever you hear is eventually what you birth. The ear is one of the gateways to the mind. You will act on and become what you hear. Faith in God is a lifting force and fear is a crippling force. So, watch your gates, especially the gates to your mind. Refuse any negativity, reject anything contrary to your life's purpose and renew your mind daily by feeding it with fresh manna which is the Word of God.

> REFUSE ANY NEGATIVITY, REJECT ANYTHING CONTRARY TO YOUR LIFE'S PURPOSE AND RENEW YOUR MIND DAILY BY FEEDING IT WITH FRESH MANNA WHICH IS THE WORD OF GOD

*"But when Sanballat the Horonite, Tobiah the Ammonite official, and Geshem the Arab heard of it, **they laughed at us and despised us, and said, 'what is this thing that you are doing?** Will you rebel against the king?'"* **(Nehemiah 2:19).**

The Sanballat Spirit

The Sanballat spirit is an adversarial spirit; it is a judgmental, deriding, distracting, defaming and deceptive spirit, whose aim is to stop the work of God in your life and in your hands. It employs physical, psychological, and emotional means to carry out its sinister work. Sanballat used at least seven strategies to stop Israel's project.

1. Derision (Nehemiah 2:10, 19)
2. Defiance (Nehemiah 4:1-8)
3. Distraction and Diversion (Nehemiah 6:1-4)
4. Defamation (Nehemiah 6:5-9)
5. Deception (Nehemiah 6:10-14)
6. Dissension (Nehemiah 6:16-19)
7. Debasement (Nehemiah 13:4-8)

Derision

Mockery and ridicule are weapons of attack on the mind. It is difficult to ignore people having a *feast of jesting* at one's expense. Mockery is hard to overlook. *"They laughed at us and despised us"* **(Nehemiah 2:19).**

> *"1But it so happened, when Sanballat heard that we were rebuilding the wall, that he was furious and very indignant and mocked the Jews. 2And he spoke before his brethren and the army of Samaria, and said, 'What are these feeble Jews doing? Will they fortify themselves? Will they offer sacrifices? Will they complete it in a day? Will they revive the stones from the heaps of rubbish stones that are burned?' 3Now Tobiah the Ammonite was beside him, and he said,*

'Whatever they build, if even a fox goes up on it, he will break down their stone wall'" (Nehemiah 4:1-3).

Distraction and Diversion

" .... that Sanballat and Geshem sent to me, saying, 'Come, let us meet together among the villages in the plain of Ono.' But they thought to do me harm" (Nehemiah 6:2).

Diversionary tactics are used to derail and silence a purpose. Sanballat hoped to divert the attention of Nehemiah and the children of Israel from their work, his unkind actions were meant to interfere with their focus.

Keep Your Focus

One of the reasons for defeat in any enterprise is loss of focus. Distraction is one of the tactical methods employed at war to shift an opponent's focus. And whenever focus is lost; the power to pursue purpose is dissipated, resolve is weakened, and failure is the ultimate outcome. An old adage says, *"If you want to defeat them, distract them."* Paying attention to less important things in critical situations is always dangerous. As the steering wheel turns the tires on a car, a shift in focus turns attention and concentration elsewhere.

> AS THE STEERING WHEEL TURNS THE TIRES ON A CAR, A SHIFT IN FOCUS TURNS ATTENTION AND CONCENTRATION ELSEWHERE

Regarding focus Henry Ford once said, *"Obstacles are those frightful things you see when you take your eyes off your goal."* You cannot achieve your goals when your eyes are off them, and you will never subdue an enemy you lose sight of. The greatest battle you will ever fight is the battle of focus. There are many people and things in life that will try to shift your focus. A shift in focus will replace your plans, change your direction and alter your destiny. When you forget where you wanted to go, and why you wanted to go there and how you planned to get there, then you have lost your focus. Sanballat used diversionary strategies to distract Nehemiah and the children of Israel from their work.

> THE GREATEST BATTLE YOU WILL EVER FIGHT IS THE BATTLE OF FOCUS

Stay Your Course

Undermining and hurtful words from people can become a distraction when too much attention is given to them. Treat every unkind word as you would treat junk mail, refuse them. Life, just like a highway, offers many exits, but as a traveler you know in order to reach your destination you cannot try every exit. Unsolicited suggestions, attractive offers, and persistent invitations are like exits on the highway of life. It is up to you to avoid unplanned exits and keep going

> UNDERMINING AND HURTFUL WORDS FROM PEOPLE CAN BECOME A DISTRACTION WHEN TOO MUCH ATTENTION IS GIVEN TO THEM. TREAT EVERY UNKIND WORD AS YOU WOULD TREAT JUNK MAIL, REFUSE THEM.

in the direction of your destination Try to remember this acronym for focus:

Fix your eyes
On your
Course
Until you
Succeed

Defamation

It is amazing how most of us can deal with people not speaking to us but find it difficult to deal with people speaking bad about us.

> *"⁵ Then Sanballat sent his servant to me as before, the fifth time, with an open letter in his hand. ⁶ In it was written:* **"It is reported among the nations, and Geshem says, that you and the Jews plan to rebel; therefore, according to these rumors, you are rebuilding the wall, that you may be their king. ⁷ And you have also appointed prophets to proclaim concerning you at Jerusalem, saying, 'There is a king in Judah!'** *Now these matters will be reported to the king. So, come, therefore, and let us consult together." ⁸ Then I sent to him, saying,* **"No such things as you say are being done, but you invent them in your own heart." ⁹ For they all were trying to make us afraid, saying, "Their hands will be weakened in the work, and it will not be done."** *Now therefore, O God, strengthen my hands"* **(Nehemiah 6:5-9).**

Unkind words, slanderous rumors, assorted lies, and fabrications about our character provokes a psychological response from us. Sanballat used defamation and denouncement tactics, along with threatening words to disturb the peace of the people and pressure them into giving up their work of rebuilding the wall.

The Secret to Fulfilling Purpose

"So, we built the wall, and the entire wall was joined together up to half its height, for the people had a mind to work" (Nehemiah 4:6).

Nehemiah and the Children of Israel finished their God given task because they refused to let Sanballat's evil machinations derail their purpose. They set their minds on their assignment and did not let discouraging words stop their God given assignment.

THE SECRET TO FULFILLING PURPOSE IS TO STAY FOCUS ON YOUR GOALS AND NEVER STOP WORKING TOWARDS YOUR PURPOSE AND MORE IMPORTANTLY TO ASK GOD FOR STRENGTH

The secret to fulfilling purpose is to stay focus on your goals and never stop working towards your purpose and more importantly to ask God for strength. Nehemiah leaves us examples on how to deal with unkind treatments from people. Nehemiah refused to be distracted from his purpose, he replied to Sanballat and said,

"I am doing a great work, so that I cannot come down. Why should the work cease while I leave it and go down to you?" (Nehemiah 6:3).

In other words, I am busy doing a great work (my life's assignment) and I am so occupied with it that I cannot spare a minute to meddle in affairs unrelated to my purpose. It wouldn't make sense at all for me to do so. It is as if you were to call me to get off my northbound train to join you for a little chat on your southbound train. I would be trading off my destination if I should concede to your invitation. Determination and focus are ingredients for fulfilling life's purpose.

> IF YOU DON'T KNOW WHERE YOU ARE GOING, YOU ARE ALREADY THERE, AND THAT IS NOWHERE!
> PEOPLE WHO DON'T KNOW THEIR LIFE'S PURPOSE OR WILL NOT STAY IN THEIR LANE ARE BOUND TO MEET WITH SOME MISFORTUNE

If you don't know where you are going, you are already there, and that is nowhere! People who do not know their life's purpose or will not stay in their lane are bound to meet with some misfortune.

> DETERMINATION AND FOCUS ARE INGREDIENTS FOR FULFILLING LIFE'S PURPOSE

One of the benefits of freewill is the power of choice, the ability to choose. It is a personal power, and with it also comes the "power of refusal" the ability to say "no" to unwanted solicitations. You can say 'no'; it is your prerogative.

Unkind words can induce anger, and anger can lead to self-defeating behaviors. Also, fear-inducing and undermining words can cause you to abandon your dreams and consequently, leave you feeling unaccomplished.

The Impact of Unkind Words is Compared to the Damage and Wounds from A Sword, a Spear or an Arrow.

"The words of the reckless pierce like swords, but the tongue of the wise brings healing" **(Proverbs 12:18 NIV).**

Words Can Cut Like Swords, Stab Like Spears and Pierce like Arrows

*"My soul is among lions; I lie among the sons of men who are set on fire, **whose teeth are spears and arrows, and their tongue a sharp sword**" (Psalm 57:4).*

*"Who have **sharpened their tongues like a sword.** They **aim venomous words as arrows**" (Psalm 64:3 AMP).*

Words Can Be as Poisonous as the Snake Venom

"They sharpen their tongues like a serpent; The poison of asps is under their lips" **(Psalm 140:3).**

Lying Tongues Can Do Damage as Arrows from a Bow

"They make ready their tongue like a bow, to shoot lies" **(Jeremiah 9:3a NIV).**

The Unbridled Tongue

CHAPTER 5

"Even so the tongue is a little member and boasts great things. See how great a forest a little fire kindles!"
(James 3:5).

The Unbridled Tongue

*"3 Indeed, we put bits in horses' mouths that they may obey us, and we turn their whole body. 4 Look also at ships: although they are so large and are driven by fierce winds, they are turned by a very small rudder wherever the pilot desires. 5 Even so the tongue is a little member and boasts great things. See how great a forest a little fire kindles! 6 And the tongue is a fire, a world of iniquity. The tongue is so set among our members that it defiles the whole body and sets on fire the course of nature; and it is set on fire by hell. 7 **For every kind of beast and bird, of reptile and creature of the sea, is tamed and has been tamed by mankind. 8 But no man can tame the tongue.** It is an unruly evil, full of deadly poison. 9 With it we bless our God and Father, and with it we curse men, who have been made in the similitude of God. 10 Out of the same mouth proceed blessing and cursing. My brethren, these things ought not to be so. 11 Does a spring send forth fresh water and bitter from the same opening? 12 Can a fig tree, my brethren, bear olives, or a grapevine bear fig? Thus, no spring yields both salt water and fresh"* (**James 3:3-12**).

THE UNBRIDLED TONGUE IS a sign of one area of life that is not yet conquered by redeeming grace. The repetition of the subject of discipline and control of speech throughout the Book of James shows the inseparable link between speech and religion (practical faith). First in James 1:19, the Apostle admonishes us all to "be swift to hear, and slow to speak" and in chapter 3:4, he explains that as the tight rein on horses control their direction, right governing of the tongue will control a man's whole behavior. In chapter 4:11, he admonishes the believer to be careful not to speak evil or judge one another and finally in chapter 5:9 and 12, he warns not to grumble against one another.

The Destructive Power of the Tongue

> *⁵Even so the tongue is a little member and boasts great things. **See how great a forest a little fire kindles!"*** **(James 3:2-5).**

On July 23, 2018, California experienced one of the largest fires in the history of the state. The devastating wildfire, (The Carr Fire) engulfed more than 207,000 acres (an area larger than New York City), destroyed more than 1,000 homes in and around Redding (a town 200 miles north of San Francisco and home to about 90,000 residents), and killed at least seven people. This vicious wildfire was caused by a mere spark from the rim of a trailer after having a flat tire. How true are the words of the Scriptures, " ... *Consider what a great forest is set on fire by a small spark"* **(James 3:5b NIV).**

"The tongue also is a fire ...."

> " ***The tongue also is a fire***, *a world of evil among the parts of the body.* ***It corrupts the whole body, sets the whole course of one's life on fire***, *and is itself set on fire by hell"* **(James 3:6 NIV).**

The tongue, like fire, is both useful and a necessity. Without the tongue we are not able to express our opinions or share our feelings; the success of all our dealings from domestic to corporate relations is dependent on good communications. Fire, just like the tongue, is necessary for living; with fire we are able to cook our food, light up a dark night, and warm our bodies. We have harnessed the power of fire in more advanced ways to greatly improve our lives in many areas. Fire, like the tongue, does irreparable damage when out of control. The key is control. If we control fire, we can use it for our own good and if we can control our tongues, we can use its power to bless God and to benefit others.

> FIRE, LIKE THE TONGUE, DOES IRREPARABLE DAMAGE WHEN OUT OF CONTROL .... IF WE CONTROL FIRE, WE CAN USE IT FOR OUR OWN GOOD AND IF WE CAN CONTROL OUR TONGUES, WE CAN USE ITS POWER TO BLESS GOD AND TO BENEFIT OTHERS.

The Perfect Man

*"For we all stumble in many things. **If anyone does not stumble in word, he is a perfect man**, able also to bridle the whole body"* **(James 3:2).**

The word translated perfect here is the Greek word *"Teleios"* and it does not mean without fault, but rather means full grown, coming to maturity from going through the necessary stages to reach an end goal. The root word *'tel'* means reaching the end. It is well illustrated with the old pirate's telescopes which unfolds, extending one

> THE MAN WHO HAS CONTROL OVER HIS WORDS IS NEAR A PERFECT MAN, THAT IS MATURED AND FULLY GROWN FROM GOING THROUGH THE NECESSARY STAGES OF SELF-DISCIPLINE THAT GIVES HIM CONTROL OVER HIS WORDS

stage at a time until it reaches full length (capacity or effectiveness). The Apostle James tells us what we already know that we are all imperfect because we stumble in many areas of our lives. However, he said the man who has control over his words is near a perfect man, that is matured and fully grown from going

> THE ONE WHO CLAIMS TO BE RELIGIOUS BUT FAILS TO SHOW IT BY WHOLESOME SPEECH (NOT BRIDLING HIS TONGUE) DECEIVES HIS OWN HEART

through the necessary stages of self-discipline that gives him control over his words.

A Worthless Religion

"If you claim to be religious but don't control your tongue, you are fooling yourself, and your religion is worthless" **(James 1:26 NLT).**

What is your religion (practical faith) worth? The Apostle James says, it is worth nothing if you do not have a disciplined tongue. Your words and actions are the spiritual barometer of your faith. Practical faith is useless without virtue and self-control. Apostle Peter also adds,

> *" 5But also for this very reason, giving all diligence,* **add to your faith virtue, to virtue knowledge,** *6 to* **knowledge self-control,** *to self-control perseverance, to perseverance godliness"* **(2 Peter 1:5-6).**

According to James the first effect of an unbridled tongue is on the individual. The one who claims to be religious but fails to show it by wholesome speech (not bridling his tongue) deceives his own heart. The liar or slanderer in his attempt to deceive others first deceives himself because only he knows the truth. The reward of the unbridled tongue is first on the individual. Jesus said, if you judge or condemn others unfairly you will be judged with the same measure.

> "¹Do not judge and criticize and condemn [others unfairly with an attitude of self-righteous superiority as though assuming the office of a judge], so that you will not be judged [unfairly]. ² **For just as you [hypocritically] judge others [when you are sinful and unrepentant], so will you be judged; and in accordance with your standard of measure [used to pass out judgment]**, judgment will be measured to you" **(Matthew 7:1-2 AMP).**

True religion will produce thoughts and actions consistent with the Word of God. Anyone hearing the Word of God must also be a doer of the Word (James 1:22). The second effect of an unbridled tongue is that the man's religion (practical faith) is worthless. Though a man's service may be that of the most noble works of charity and Christian service, if the same man knows

TRUE RELIGION WILL PRODUCE THOUGHTS AND ACTIONS CONSISTENT WITH THE WORD OF GOD

nothing of wholesome speech, all his labors in the name of religion are useless. One should pay attention that the tongue is not destroying that which the hands are building, because it is possible to destroy with the tongue in a moment what has taken the hands a lifetime to build.

Should You Really Say Everything You are Thinking?

There are those who boast about the fact that they say whatever is on their mind and do not care that their words may be hurtful or damaging to other people's feelings. It is impossible to avoid being offended or meet with upsetting situations that calls for response, but the way you react or respond in heated moments shows the level of self-discipline and mastery you have

> IT IS EASIER TO BLURT OUT WITH EXPLOSIVE WORDS THAN TO BE QUITE OR RESPOND GRACEFULLY

developed over your tongue. It is easier to blurt out with explosive words than to be quiet or respond gracefully.

> *"Those who control their tongue will have a long life; opening your mouth can ruin everything"* (Proverbs 13:3 NLT).

The Problem with the Unbridled Tongue

The problem with unbridled tongue is that it is rooted in our inherent nature (the sinful nature). Unwholesome speech is not just a sign of an undisciplined life, but a proof of the fallen nature. The Bible is full of admonitions to develop a disciplined tongue and warnings against unhealthy and unkind words and further maintains that

> UNWHOLESOME WORDS ARE NOT JUST SIGN OF AN UNDISCIPLINED LIFE, BUT A PROOF OF THE FALLEN NATURE

a disciplined tongue is proof of true religion, while it negates the religion of the man who has no control over his tongue. Therefore, an unbridled tongue is a spiritual problem and needs a spiritual solution. It will take divine help to overcome the danger and the natural propensity of the tongue.

The Pharisees and the religious scholars came to Jesus to report and charged His disciples with violating the tradition of the elders. They noted that the disciples of Jesus did not observe the ceremonial washing of hands before they ate, and to do so was considered defilement.

Jesus knowing well that the Pharisees paid a lot of attention to the externals (outward religiosity), but neglected fundamental issues that really mattered to God, replied the Pharisees in this manner:

> *"It's not what goes into your mouth that defiles you; you are defiled by the words that come out of your mouth"* **(Matthew 15:11 NLT).**

He explained to the crowd that whatever goes in through the mouth does not defile a man, but only what comes out of the mouth defiles the man, because what comes out of the mouth reflects the content of the heart.

How to Control the Tongue

King David understood the problem with the unbridled tongue. We read many of his prayers and resolutions concerning his words, his lips and his mouth. He resolved to watch what he says and what he does.

> *"I said to myself, 'I will watch what I do and not sin in what I say. I will hold my tongue ....'"* **(Psalm 39:1 NLT).**

Although he was king and could probably say whatever he wanted to anyone without any consequences. David was very aware of the personal responsibility of controlling his tongue and his words to others. He understood that the unbridled tongue is a spiritual problem therefore, he **prayed to God for help with his tongue.**

> *"Set a guard, O Lord, over my mouth; Keep watch over the door of my lips"* **(Psalm 141:3).**

Once more he prayed that his words and thoughts be acceptable to God and resolved to train and use his mouth to praise God and **refrain from using unkind words** to berate or dishonor men who are made in God's image. He developed a **principled lifestyle** based on God's Word with **continuous prayer** for strength in this area. David formed a habit of **speaking kind words** even to his enemies.

> *"Let the words of my mouth and the meditation of my heart be acceptable in Your sight, O Lord, my strength and my Redeemer"* **(Psalm 19:14).**
>
> *"And my tongue shall speak of Your righteousness and of Your praise all day long"* **(Psalm 35:28).**
>
> *"I will sing of the mercies of the Lord forever; with my mouth will I make known Your faithfulness to all generations"* **(Psalm 89:1).**

In addition to prayer, the following **physical exercises** can help prevent you from saying things you might later regret during heated moments. These suggestions are based on two major rules: (1) delaying your response and

(2) distracting from the anger. Before you speak, remember to calm down, count down, count the cost and consider it, but say it not.

1. **Calm Down**: Your ability to reason logically and communicate effectively is impaired by the emotion of anger. Anger reflects a lack of poise. So, in heated moments, try to calm down and get a hold of yourself; this way you are sure to communicate your message rather than your anger.

2. **Count Down**: Pause before you respond. Take time out, count down from 10 to 1.

3. **Count the Cost**: Think about the consequences of your words. Once you have spoken, you will not be able to take your words back.

4. **Consider it but say it not:** In heated moments it is unavoidable to have thoughts of hurtful or vengeful words, but they are better not spoken.

How to Control the Tongue (Recap)

- **Pray to God for help with the tongue.
Refrain from using unkind words**
- **Develop a principled lifestyle** based on God's Word with **continuous prayer** for strength.
- **Practice speaking kind words.**
- **Practice physical restraints exercises.**

Making Your Words Count

CHAPTER 6

"Watch the way you talk. Let nothing foul or dirty come out of your mouth. Say only what helps, each word a gift"
(Ephesians 4:29 MSG).

THE BIBLE TALKS ABOUT a day in which we must give account of all the careless words we have spoken. Are you ready to face your words?

Are You Ready to Face Your Words?

*"Let me tell you something: **Every one of these careless words is going to come back to haunt you. There will be a time of reckoning. Words are powerful; take them seriously. Words can be your salvation. Words can also be your damnation"*** (Matthew 12:36-37 MSG).

It is understandable why God will judge blasphemies and profanities, but most people find it surprising that God will also judge every careless word men may speak. The word translated careless here also means; idle, or useless, empty, uninspiring, unedifying and lifeless. If you pleasurably indulge in idle talks, unprofitable chatters or cruel jesting, you will have to face your words someday, because the words you speak about or to people never die. Your words to your family (children, spouses, kinfolks), friends, and colleagues remain

> IF YOU PLEASURABLY INDULGE IN IDLE TALKS, UNPRODUCTIVE CHATTERS OR CRUEL JESTING, YOU WILL HAVE TO FACE YOUR WORDS SOMEDAY, BECAUSE THE WORDS YOU SPEAK...... NEVER DIE

with them. What a man thinks he becomes, also what a man thinks he speaks, so you are what you have said.

If your life is out of control and your relationships are always short-lived, you might want to pay attention to your words. According to Jesus we are not only accountable for speaking unkind words, but also for words that may not be bad but unprofitable to the hearers.

What Are Idle Words?

Idle words are words that do not help others, words spoken carelessly without thought or concern as to how it affects others. They are:

Gossiping Words: Words spoken to spread personal information about the life and concerns of others.

Bigoted Words: Words spoken that expresses intolerance for other people's race, creed, belief and opinions.

Censuring Words: Words spoken that expresses strong disapproval or harsh criticism of others.

Angry Words: Words spoken angrily to others.

Blame Shifting Words: Words spoken to make others responsible for one's personal mistakes or problems.

Demeaning Words: Words spoken that berates and smear the character of others.

Envious Words: Words spoken out of envy or jealousy.

Hurtful Words: Words spoken that inflict hurt or pain to others (injurious words).

Prideful Words: Words spoken in pride. Words that belittle others and exalts self. Sometimes prideful words may be spoken with false humility.
Deceitful Words: Words spoken to mislead others.

Making Your Words Count

".... Let nothing foul or dirty come out of your mouth.
Say only what helps..." (Ephesians 4:29 MSG).

Making your words count starts with the heart, **the heart must be renewed.** If the heart is not kind the tongue will tell it. If there is no snow on the mountain, there will be drought in the plain. Kind people are known by their words (kind words) and their deeds (kindness).

How to Renew the Heart

The heart is like the soil. To have a healthy plant and a bountiful crop, the condition of the soil must be right. The condition of the heart must be right to have wholesome speech. If the soil is too acidic, certain plants find it difficult to thrive because their ability to absorb nutrients is impaired in an acidic soil. It is possible to treat the soil and reverse this condition by neutralizing the acidity of the soil to a more favorable soil pH.

> IF THE HEART IS NOT KIND THE TONGUE WILL TELL IT. IF THERE IS NO SNOW ON THE MOUNTAIN, THERE WILL BE DROUGHT IN THE PLAIN

The heart, like the soil must be renewed; unwholesome speech is not just a result of social influence and personal breeding, but a moral and spiritual problem. All through the ages, men have realized the depravity of the heart, and prayed to God for a renewed heart. David prayed this way,

> *"Create in me a clean heart, O God, and renew a right and steadfast spirit within me"* **(Psalm 51:10 AMP).**

Unless there is a new heart, a new spirit or a clean heart there can be no wholesome speech. The streams are bitter when the fountain is poisoned. Like David, **one must ask God for a new heart and a fresh start.** God himself promised to give a new heart.

> *"And I will give you a new heart, and I will put a new spirit in you. I will take out your stony, stubborn heart and give you a tender, responsive heart"* **(Ezekiel 36:26 NLT).**

A fresh start means a new way of thinking and living. The heart must be cultivated anew. Paying careful attention to the welfare of the heart to ensure that the heart is free of negativity. And like the soil the heart's environment must not be toxic. Intentional living begins when one takes control of the thought life.

AND LIKE THE SOIL THE HEART'S ENVIRONMENT MUST NOT BE TOXIC. INTENTIONAL LIVING BEGINS WHEN ONE TAKES CONTROL OF THE THOUGHT LIFE

Paul the Apostle offered this time-tested instructions on how to safeguard the heart and emotions:

> *"Finally, believers, **whatever is true, whatever is honorable** and **worthy of respect, whatever is***

> right *and* confirmed *by God's word,* whatever is
> pure *and* wholesome, *whatever is* lovely *and* brings
> peace, *whatever is* admirable *and of good repute; if*
> there is any excellence, *if there is* anything worthy of
> praise, think continually on these things *[center*
> your mind on them, and implant them in your
> heart]" **(Philippians 4:8 AMP).**

When the mind is filled with wholesome thoughts, it will show in communications with others; and until then, we cannot make our words count.

Also, in order to make your words count, you will need to **practice speaking only words that improve others;** this will take time, but like everything else, practice makes perfect.

Finally, **practice listening more than talking** to others. You and I are advised to listen more to people than trying to talk to them. *"LISTEN and SILENT are spelled with the same letters, think about it."* Try to be silent and listen to your friends, it may be the best gift other than time you will ever give to them. If you listen well, you will respond well. If you listen well, you will be able to make your words count. Listening is an indispensable ingredient in securing happy and successful relationships.

> HEARING IS NOT THE SAME AS LISTENING, HEARING TELLS YOU A SONG IS PLAYING, BUT LISTENING TELL YOU WHAT SONG IS PLAYING

Hearing is not the same as listening; hearing tells you a song is playing, but listening tell you what song is playing.

"Understand this, my beloved brothers and sisters. **Let everyone be quick to hear [be a careful, thoughtful listener], slow to speak [a speaker of carefully chosen words and],** *slow to anger [patient, reflective, forgiving]"* **(James 1:19 AMP).**

Your Words Reflect Your Heart

"You have minds like a snake pit! How do you suppose what you say is worth anything when you are so foul-minded? **It's your heart, not the dictionary, that gives meaning to your words. A good person produces good deeds and words season after season.** *An evil person is a blight on the orchard"* **(Matthew 12:35 MSG).**

Whatever is coming out of your mouth reveal the condition of your heart. There is a link between the tongue and the heart, one reflects the other. The tongue is ruled by the heart, for *"Out of the abundance of the heart the mouth speaks."* Therefore, an evil tongue is a result of an evil heart.

Your words reveal what you think of others and paint the image you have created of them in your heart. Your words also reveal your own nature. It may reveal how kind and wise you are or how cruel and foolish you are. Words are first conceived in the heart before they are spoken by the mouth. *"The fool has said in his heart, "There is no God ...."* (Psalm 14:1a). So, what is the state of your heart?

> YOUR WORDS REVEAL WHAT YOU THINK OF OTHERS AND PAINT THE IMAGE YOU HAVE CREATED OF THEM IN YOUR HEART YOUR WORDS ALSO REVEAL YOUR OWN NATURE.

"17Do you not yet understand that whatever enters the mouth goes into the stomach and is eliminated? 18 But those things which proceed out of the mouth come from the heart, and they defile a man. 19 For out of the heart proceed evil thoughts, murders, adulteries, fornications, thefts, false witness, blasphemies" **(Matthew 15:17-19).**

The Heart is a Reservoir

"Above all else, guard your heart, for everything you do flows from it" **(Proverbs 4:23 NIV).**

The heart is a storehouse just like a reservoir, and it is the wellsprings of life. Reservoirs are the source of water supply to several thousand homes in many cities of the world. Drinking water regulations require that townships maintain strict quality control procedures to protect reservoirs from unauthorized access and assure that stored water in reservoirs are not contaminated by entry of animals, birds, insects, dust and other potential sources of contamination. Just like the water reservoir, you must also guard and protect your heart from all forms of contaminations and deny access to every unsolicited thoughts and suggestions. An uncluttered mind is an uncluttered life.

> GUARD AND PROTECT YOUR HEART FROM ALL FORMS OF CONTAMINATIONS AND DENY ACCESS TO EVERY UNSOLICITED THOUGHTS AND SUGGESTIONS. AN UNCLUTTERED MIND IS AN UNCLUTTERED LIFE

THE POWER OF KIND WORDS

Each Word a Gift

*" Watch the way you talk. Let nothing foul or dirty come out of your mouth. **Say only what helps, each word a gift"** (Ephesians 4:29 MSG).*

How wonderful it is to know that each word can be a gift for the hearer. Imagine what our world would be if we all understood this simple but powerful concept; we may then harness the power that can change the world for good.

> HOW WONDERFUL IT IS TO KNOW THAT EACH WORD CAN BE A GIFT FOR THE HEARER

The giving and exchanging of gifts brings so much joy around the holidays, as we all share in the "joy of gifting", but we can experience the same joy every day, if we give the gift of kind words in our daily conversations and interactions with people. Don't forget every word can be a gift.

The Admonition to Build Each Other Up with Kind Words

The Bible is filled with commands to be considerate of others and be intentional in speaking only words that uplift and build others up. Kind and comforting words are deliberate words. Therefore, choose to lift someone else up with your words. Make it a practice to

> MAKE IT A PRACTICE TO GIVE COMPLIMENTS WHENEVER THEY ARE DUE, ... LIGHT UP YOUR SPACE, LIFT A DROOPING HEAD, BRIGHTEN UP A SAD FACE. RELEASE THE POWER OF KIND WORDS

give compliments whenever they are due, find something

good to say about others, light up your space, lift a drooping head, brighten up a sad face. Release the power of kind words and make the world a better place.

> *"Therefore* **encourage one another and build up one another,** *just as you also are doing"* **(1 Thessalonians 5:11 NASB).**

> *"And* **let us consider one another** *to provoke unto love and to good works"* **(Hebrews 10:24 KJV).**
> *"So, then we pursue the things which make for peace* **and the building up of one another"** *(Romans* **14:19 NASB).**

> *"***Judas and Silas,** *who themselves were prophets,* **said much to encourage and strengthen the brothers"** **(Acts 15:32 BSB-Berean Study Bible).**

> *"Let your speech always be with grace, seasoned with salt,* *that you may know how you ought to answer each one"* **(Colossians 4:6).**

> *"Therefore comfort one another with these words"* **(1 Thessalonians 4:18).**

How to Make Your Words Count (Recap)

To make your words count you will need to:

- **Renew your heart.**
- **Practice speaking only words that improve others.**
- **Practice listening more than talking to others.**

The Kind Words of Jesus

CHAPTER 7

"So, all bore witness to Him and marveled at the words which proceeded out of His mouth. And they said, "Is this not Joseph's son?"
(Luke 4:22)

THE KIND WORDS OF JESUS

THERE HAS BEEN NO ONE whose words were so gracious, so kind and most re-assuring as Jesus. His words were not only kind but life-giving. For instance, He said, *"The words that I speak to you are Spirit and life"* (John 6:63). Also, he said, *"I am come that they might have life"* (John 10:10). Many who met Him during His ministry were deeply impacted by His kind words. The Gospel is full of His encounters with many who were objects of His mercy. Here are a few of those life changing encounters.

The Woman at the Well

Jesus knowing this woman's shameful past, and her present illicit relationship was very kind to her. He spoke not one word of condemnation to her, but instead helped her to realize the true longing of her heart. He commended her for her honesty and revealed Himself as the Messiah she knew was coming.

> *"7A woman of Samaria came to draw water. Jesus said to her, "Give Me a drink. 8For His disciples had gone away into the city to buy food. 9Then the woman of Samaria said to Him, "How is it that You, being a Jew, ask a drink from me, a Samaritan woman?" For Jews have no dealings with Samaritans. 10**Jesus answered and said to her, "If you knew the gift of God, and who it is who says to you, 'Give Me a drink,' you would have asked Him, and He would have given you living water."** ....15The woman said to Him, **"Sir, give me this water, that I may not thirst, nor come here to draw."** 16Jesus said to her, "Go, call your husband, and come here." 17The woman answered and said, "I have no husband." Jesus*

said to her, "You have well said, 'I have no husband,' [18]*for you have had five husbands, and the one whom you now have is not your husband; in that you spoke truly…...*[25]*The woman said to Him,* **"I know that Messiah is coming (who is called Christ). When He comes, He will tell us all things."** [26]*Jesus said to her, **"I who speak to you am He"*** **(John 4:7-10, 15-18, 25-26).**

The Woman Caught in Adultery

In just a few minutes this woman would have been stoned to death. Her accusers held in their hands stones to condemn her; they were only awaiting her damnation from Jesus. This nameless, helpless woman was drowning in a sea of guilt and shame, sinking to rise no more but then just in time a hand lifted her. Jesus' words to her accusers stopped them and His kind words to her saved her.

This was Jesus in action, the embodiment of God's love and grace. The Bible says of Him, *"And of His fullness we have all received, and grace for grace"* **(John 1:16).**

"[7]* So when they continued asking Him, He raised Himself up and said to them,* **"He who is without sin among you, let him throw a stone at her first."** [8] *And again He stooped down and wrote on the ground.* [9] *Then those who heard it, being convicted by their conscience, went out one by one, beginning with the oldest even to the last. And Jesus was left alone, and the woman standing in the midst.* [10] *When Jesus had raised Himself up and saw no one but the woman, He said to her,* **"Woman, where are those accusers of yours? Has no one condemned you?"** [11] *She said, "No one, Lord." And Jesus said to her,* **"Neither do I condemn you; go and sin no more."** [12] *Then Jesus spoke to them again, saying,* **"I am the**

light of the world. He who follows Me shall not walk in darkness but have the light of life" **(John 8:7-12).**

The Blind Man

This man had been healed of his blindness without knowing who his benefactor was. The blind man was immensely happy but didn't know who Jesus was; he was profoundly grateful but didn't know who to thank until Jesus found him. His healing had become the subject of religious and political controversy and this man was unsure why his healing had caused such a great commotion. The religious leaders discounted his miracle for having occurred on the Sabbath day and treated him badly for having been fortunate on their holy day.

They eventually threw him out of the temple and when Jesus heard about his plight, He went looking for him and led him into a fuller knowledge of Himself, as the Messiah.

"35 Jesus heard that they had cast him out; and when He had found him, He said to him, "Do you believe in the Son of God?" 36 He answered and said, "Who is He, Lord, that I may believe in Him?" 37 And Jesus said to him, "You have both seen Him and it is He who is talking with you." 38 Then he said, "Lord, I believe!" And he worshiped Him" **(John 9:35-38).**

Mary and Martha

This is one of many stories that clearly show that we do not only have a Savior who cares, but also a friend in Jesus.

In one moment, He cried with the bereaved sisters and in the next moment He raised their dead brother. But why did He cry, if He was going to raise the dead man? It was because Jesus felt the sorrow of this grief-stricken family.

The Jews that were present all witnessed this amazing display of compassion and they remarked, *"See how He loved him!"* He quieted their hearts from all baffling thoughts and told them to trust in God in this difficult time. In moments like these Jesus comes to us and offers us hope and speaks words of comfort to us.

> *"32 Then, when Mary came where Jesus was, and saw Him, she fell down at His feet, saying to Him, "Lord, if You had been here, my brother would not have died." 33 Therefore, when Jesus saw her weeping, and the Jews who came with her weeping, He groaned in the spirit and was troubled. 34 And He said, "Where have you laid him?" They said to Him, "Lord, come and see." 35* **Jesus wept**. *36 Then the Jews said, "See how He loved him!" ....* **40 Jesus said to her, "Did I not say to you that if you would believe you would see the glory of God?" .... 43 Now when He had said these things, He cried with a loud voice, "Lazarus, come forth!"** *(John 11:32-36, 40, 43).*

Mary of Bethany

> *"3 Then Mary took a pound of very costly oil of spikenard, anointed the feet of Jesus, and wiped His feet with her hair. And the house was filled with the fragrance of the oil. "4 But one of His disciples, Judas Iscariot, Simon's son, who would betray Him, said, 5 "Why was this fragrant oil not sold for three hundred denarii and given to the poor?" 6 This he said, not that he cared for the poor, but because he was a thief, and had the money box;*

and he used to take what was put in it. ⁷ **But Jesus said, "Let her alone; she has kept this for the day of My burial"** (John 12:3-7).

Like a man on death row knows when and how he will die, the Lord's heart was filled with the thought of his impending death. He came into the house of his friends in Bethany for company. In times like these everyone need trusted friends. As He sat in the house, Mary unexpectedly began to anoint his feet and wipe them with her hair and the house was filled with the fragrance of the oil.

This action of Mary was criticized by Judas, one of the Lord's disciples as a waste of this costly oil that could have been sold and the money given to the poor. However, Jesus defended Mary and acknowledged her gift. Mary's gift to Jesus was an expression of her worship.

According to Mary true worship must be about Jesus, and it mustn't be cheap, but extravagant. Mary's action was defended by the Lord, *"Let her alone; she has kept this for the day of My burial"* (John 12:7). Mary's gift was spirit-led in the sense that the

> MANY OF US MISS OUR MOMENTS TO GIVE OUR LOVED ONES THEIR FLOWERS WHEN THEY CAN SMELL THEM, INSTEAD WAIT TO PLACE IT ON THEIR CASKETS WHEN THEY CANNOT SMELL THEM. WHATEVER YOU NEED TO DO FOR JESUS, DO IT NOW

resurrection of Christ makes the anointing and embalming unnecessary. There was no opportunity for the others to anoint Him because by the time they got to the tomb on the third day, He had risen.

So, Mary's anointing of Jesus was intuitive, insightful, and timely. Many of us miss our moments to give our loved ones their flowers when they can smell them, instead of waiting to place it on their caskets when they cannot smell them. Whatever you need to do for Jesus, do it now.

His Mother

There is no pain a mother cannot not endure except the pain of feeling helpless while her child suffers. Mary, the Mother of Jesus, stood at the cross with such indescribable sorrow as she observed her dying son, there was nothing she could do for Him now. Amid all of this, Jesus himself feeling His mother's pain and knowing she would need comfort and care arranged for John, one of his disciples, to take over the custody of His mother.

This was one of the most remarkable things any son ever had done for a mother. Most people do not have the capacity to think of other people's welfare during their own pain. Despite the terrible and painful situation Jesus was in, He made no excuse to neglecting his mother's care. A very clear example for us all.

> *"26 When Jesus therefore saw His mother, and the disciple whom He loved standing by, He said to His mother,* **"Woman, behold your son!"** *27 Then He said to the disciple, "Behold your mother!" And from that hour that disciple took her to his own home"* **(John 19:26-27).**

Thomas

> *"26And after eight days His disciples were again inside, and Thomas with them. Jesus came, the doors being shut,*

and stood in the midst, and said, "Peace to you!" [27] *Then He said to Thomas, "Reach your finger here, and look at My hands; and reach your hand here and put it into My side.* **Do not be unbelieving but believing."** [28] **And Thomas answered and said to Him, "My Lord and my God!"** (John 20:26-28).

At a time when the disciples needed each other's company for strength and comfort, it is surprising and quite suspicious that any one of them would try to find strength in solace. The Bible is silent as to where Thomas was, but wherever he was could not have been the right place for him at the time. Let us learn that it is unhelpful for us to keep away from assembling with the other believers. When we do, we miss opportunities and the Lord's visitation among the congregation, and we also become out of step with the Holy Spirit's move in the church. However, Jesus' words to Thomas were kind and gentle, instead of condemning his unbelief, He encouraged his belief.

LET US LEARN THAT IT IS UNHELPFUL FOR US TO KEEP AWAY FROM THE ASSEMBLING WITH THE OTHER BELIEVERS. WHEN WE DO, WE MISS OPPORTUNITIES AND THE LORD'S VISITATION AMONG THE CONGREGATION AND WE ALSO BECOME OUT OF STEP WITH THE HOLY SPIRIT'S MOVE IN THE CHURCH

Peter

Just a few hours before Jesus was arrested, Jesus warned Peter of his impeding temptation and Satan's plan to derail his destiny, but Jesus assured him, *"I have prayed for you."*

*" 31And the Lord said, "Simon, Simon! Indeed, **Satan has asked for you, that he may sift you as wheat. 32 But I have prayed for you, that your faith should not fail;** and when you have returned to Me, strengthen your brethren."* **(Luke 22:31-32).**

After Peter had denied that he ever knew Jesus, his courage was gone, and he felt very disappointed with himself and became unsure of his future as a disciple of Jesus. A series of events happened that changed everything for Peter. First, it was a personal message to Peter from the Lord delivered by the Angel to the disciples who went to the grave.

*"6 But he said to them, "Do not be alarmed. You seek Jesus of Nazareth, who was crucified. He is risen! He is not here. See the place where they laid Him. 7 **But go, tell His disciples — and Peter** – that He is going before you into Galilee; there you will see Him, as He said to you"* **(Mark 16:6-7).**

And second, Jesus went to find Peter and the rest of the discouraged disciples after he had resurrected; He spoke kindly to Peter and restored him back to his call.

*"15**So when they had eaten breakfast, Jesus said to Simon Peter, "Simon, son of Jonah, do you love Me more than these?"** He said to Him, "Yes, Lord; You know that I love You." He said to him, **"Feed My lambs."** 16 He said to him again a second time, "Simon, son of Jonah, do you love Me?" He said to Him, "Yes, Lord; You know that I love You." He said to him, **"Tend My sheep."** 17 He said to him the third time, "Simon, son of Jonah, do you love Me?" Peter was grieved because He said to him the third time, "Do you love Me?" And he said to Him, "Lord, you know all*

things; You know that I love You." Jesus said to him, **"Feed My sheep"** **(John 21:15-17).**

Judas

Jesus chose Judas to be one of His disciples and loved him. It is amazing to think that up until the last-minute Jesus still regarded Judas, his betrayer, as a friend.

"48 Now His betrayer had given them a sign, saying, "Whomever I kiss, He is the One; seize Him." 49 Immediately he went up to Jesus and said, "Greetings, Rabbi!" and kissed Him. **50 But Jesus said to him, "Friend, why have you come?"** *Then they came and laid hands on Jesus and took Him"* **(Matthew 26:48-50).**

The Palsied

The palsied man was brought by four of his friends to see Jesus. They knew if the man's condition was going to change for good, he would need to meet with Jesus. They met with some obstacles, but they refused to take the friend back home the same way they brought him. This man had been in this condition for some time and must have had enough time to reflect on his lifestyle, which was the root-cause of his problems. He did not need anyone to condemn him or remind him of his past. Jesus' kind words of forgiveness to this man saved him and gave his heart hope again.

*"When He saw their faith, He said to him, **"Man, your sins are forgiven you"** (Luke 5:20).*

John the Baptist

If all the preachers around would speak well of each other and protect each other's reputation as Jesus did with John, many more pastors would survive the ministry. When John was at his lowest, Jesus sent him kind and reassuring words.

> *"24 When the messengers of John had departed, **He began to speak to the multitudes concerning John:** "What did you go out into the wilderness to see? A reed shaken by the wind? 25 But what did you go out to see? A man clothed in soft garments? Indeed, those who are gorgeously appareled and live in luxury are in kings' courts. 26 But what did you go out to see? A prophet? **Yes, I say to you, and more than a prophet.** 27 This is he of whom it is written: 'Behold, I send My messenger before Your face, who will prepare Your way before You. '28 For **I say to you, among those born of women there is not a greater prophet than John the Baptist;** but he who is least in the kingdom of God is greater than he'"* **(Luke 7:24-28).**

The Woman With the Issue of Blood

Having tried so many physicians to no avail and instead of getting well she was nothing better. She was sick and tired, destitute and despised, prevented by the law to be in public or in contact with people because of her condition, yet she pressed her way through the crowd and risked touching the holiest man on earth. If she had touched a Pharisee, it would have been death by stoning, but something within her believed she would receive mercy and love from Jesus.

She experienced a transforming grace that day. From the nameless woman *"who"* touched me, to *"somebody"* touch me, and then to *"Daughter"*. It didn't matter that we didn't know her name, her name could not have been sweeter than what Jesus called her now, "Daughter". Indeed, true faith in Jesus will change your status in life. This new status suggests a covenant relationship.

> *"45 And Jesus said, **"Who touched Me?"** When all denied it, Peter and those with him said, "Master, the multitudes throng and press You, and You say, 'Who touched Me?'"* *46 But Jesus said, **"Somebody touched Me,** for I perceived power going out from Me." 47 Now when the woman saw that she was not hidden, she came trembling; and falling down before Him, she declared to Him in the presence of all the people the reason she had touched Him and how she was healed immediately. 48 And He said to her, **"Daughter, be of good cheer, your faith has made you well. Go in peace"** (Luke 8:45-48).*

Zacchaeus

A tax collector is one of the most despised among the Jews for many reasons, one being that a devoted or patriotic Jew would not have taken this job. Zacchaeus was not just a tax collector but was chief of tax collectors and had become very rich from this ill-reputed career. Even though his lifestyle and career were questionable, one day he felt a need to meet Jesus. When he made effort to see Jesus, he was prevented by the large crowd and by his short stature, therefore, he ran ahead and up a tree, hoping that he could see Jesus. Amazingly, when Jesus reached under that tree He called out to Zacchaeus. Zacchaeus must have been shocked that Jesus stopped at all and that he knew his name without any prior introduction.

Then Zacchaeus heard the kindest words anyone had ever spoken to him. The bad reputation associated with his career had made him despised by fellow citizens and prevented him from the temple. No Pharisee would have any dealing with him, much less go to his house. So, it must have been very surprising to him that Jesus invited Himself to his home; in fact, Jesus said, *"Today I must stay at your house"* (Luke 19:5).

> IT MUST HAVE BEEN VERY SURPRISING TO HIM THAT JESUS INVITED HIMSELF TO HIS HOME; IN FACT, JESUS SAID, "TODAY I MUST STAY AT YOUR HOUSE"

These kind words gave Zacchaeus hope and extended to him the forgiveness and acceptance he longed for. *"I must stay at your house."* Jesus goes where others will not go and He makes our welfare and salvation His necessity. *"And He must needs go through Samaria"* (John 4:4 KJV). With Jesus, "He must" with everything concerning us. A sympathetic savior must save us, He must heal us, He must find us, He must deliver us, He must watch over us, and He must guide us.

> *"And when Jesus came to the place, He looked up and saw him, and said to him, "Zacchaeus, make haste and come down, for* **today I must stay at your house"** (Luke 19:5).

The Thief on the Cross

In his own words this thief dying alongside Jesus, admitted he was rightly condemned and deserved his punishment. And it is safe to infer that whatever brought him to this point must have been serious enough to warrant death by crucifixion. Also, it is certain that from the moment he was arrested, tried, condemned and now dying on the cross, he would have been subjected to scorn and ridicule and heard no kind words from anyone until now when Jesus spoke to him.

Just before he died something beautiful happened that paints a glaring picture of the very reason why Jesus was dying. Jesus said that, *"He came to seek and to save the lost"* (Luke 19:10). This thief admitted he was a sinner, repented of his sins, acknowledged Jesus as Lord and King and asked Him for admission into His Kingdom.

> *"42 Then he said to Jesus,* **"Lord, remember me** *when You come into Your kingdom."* *43 And Jesus said to him, "Assuredly, I say to you,* **today you will be with Me in Paradise"** **(Luke 23:42-43).**

Not only did Jesus answer his prayers but gave him assurance of salvation. This mercy is available to all and today.

Nicodemus

> *"1 There was a man of the Pharisees named Nicodemus, a ruler of the Jews. 2 This man came to Jesus by night and said to Him, "Rabbi, we know that You are a teacher come from God; for no one can do these signs that You do*

unless God is with him." ³ Jesus answered and said to him, "Most assuredly, I say to you, unless one is born again, he cannot see the kingdom of God." ⁴ Nicodemus said to Him, "How can a man be born when he is old? Can he enter a second time into his mother's womb and be born?" ….. ¹⁴ And as Moses lifted up the serpent in the wilderness, even so must the Son of Man be lifted up, ¹⁵ that whoever believes in Him should not perish but have eternal life. ¹⁶ For God so loved the world that He gave His only begotten Son, that whoever believes in Him should not perish but have everlasting life. ¹⁷ For God did not send His Son into the world to condemn the world, but that the world through Him might be saved" **(John 3:1-4, 14-17).**

Nicodemus was a Pharisee, and a member of the Jewish ruling council, the Sanhedrin which is the supreme council in Israel. The Pharisees had a monopoly to religious teaching in Israel and therefore were always suspecting of new teachers, especially the most famous of them all Jesus of Nazareth. They had publicly and privately showed their hatred of Jesus and planned how to get rid of this new teacher. There were a lot of disagreements about Jesus among the religious leaders in Jerusalem. Many times, they sent out representatives and spies to listen in to Jesus' teachings and other times they sent their experts to question Him, with the hope of catching Him saying something heretical or anything that might sound as libel or treason against Rome.

All their efforts had failed, and more frustrating for them were countless numbers of people across the land with proofs of the wonderful miracles they had received from Jesus. Even the Pharisees were saying among themselves,

"… You are accomplishing nothing. Look, the world has gone after Him!" (John 12:19). There was undeniable proof of His healings everywhere. They could argue about His teachings but could not deny the many miracles before them. The Pharisees themselves knew men who once walked about their streets with canes either because they were blind or lame, who can now see and walk.

Nicodemus came to Jesus because he was battling with religion and truth in his heart. His religious training and professional associates disagreed with who Jesus was. And despite what the Pharisaic caucus thought of Jesus, there were some truths about Jesus that were apparent and undeniable too much for an honest mind to discount. An old African proverb says, *"When you are crying, you can still see."* In a pool loop of bias, an honest heart can still find a drop of truth.

> NICODEMUS CAME TO JESUS BECAUSE HE WAS BATTLING WITH RELIGION AND TRUTH IN HIS HEART……. AND DESPITE WHAT THE PHARISAIC CAUCUS THOUGHT OF JESUS, THERE WERE SOME TRUTHS ABOUT JESUS THAT WERE APPARENT AND UNDENIABLE TOO MUCH FOR AN HONEST MIND TO DISCOUNT.

Nicodemus acted on the truth he knew about Jesus and came to Him. Religious bias, traditions or culture, should not stop us from examining the claims of Jesus. It took real courage for him to come to Jesus. Whereas the Pharisees were unapproachable, Nicodemus knew he could come to see Jesus. Except for the High Priest, no other Pharisee was more notable than Nicodemus during the time and ministry of Jesus. Jesus also remarked concerning Nicodemus:

"You are the [great and well-known] teacher of Israel, and yet you do not know nor understand these things [from Scripture]?" (John 3:10 AMP).

In the conversation with Jesus, it was apparent that Nicodemus could not grasp the spiritual truths Jesus was explaining to him. Nicodemus was well learned, yet there were many things he did not know; though a scholar, he did not know the truth about God's love. Men cannot understand the heart of God or spiritual matters by natural intelligence or education. The scriptures say, *"But the natural man does not receive the things of the Spirit of God, for they are foolishness to him; nor can he know them, because they are spiritually discerned"* (1 Corinthians 2:14).

> NICODEMUS ACTED ON THE TRUTH HE KNEW ABOUT JESUS AND CAME TO HIM. RELIGIOUS BIAS, TRADITIONS OR CULTURE, SHOULD NOT STOP US FROM EXAMINING THE CLAIMS OF JESUS

Everyone in Israel had a hope and was looking forward to the kingdom of God, but Jesus said to Nicodemus that, *"unless one is born again (born from above) he cannot see the kingdom of God."* Nicodemus could not understand the need for this or how it was possible for a man to be born again when he is already old. It was obvious that he could not understand the spiritual meaning of what Jesus was saying, he knew the letter of the law, but did not understand the spirit or the essence (meaning) of the scripture.

> *"He has qualified us [making us sufficient] as ministers of a new covenant [of salvation through Christ], not of the letter [of a written code] but of the Spirit; **for the letter [of the Law] kills [by revealing sin and demanding***

obedience], but the Spirit gives life" **(2 Corinthians 3:6 AMP).**

Since Nicodemus was an expert in the Old Testament scriptures, Jesus referred to the Old Testament story where Moses was instructed to raise up a bronze replica of the serpent as cure for those who were bitten by the venomous snakes in the wilderness, so that those who look up at this serpent on the pole will not die but live (Number 21:8).

> *"14 And as Moses lifted up the serpent in the wilderness, even so must the Son of Man be lifted up, 15 that whoever believes in Him should not perish but have eternal life. 16 For God so loved the world that He gave His only begotten Son, that whoever believes in Him should not perish but have everlasting life"* **(John 3:14-16).**

Jesus explained to Nicodemus that this Old Testament event was a foreshadow of redemption for all who have been bitten and laden with the venom of sin. And that He will be lifted up just as that serpent was lifted in the wilderness, and whoever put their trust in Him will not perish but will obtain eternal life. Nicodemus was hearing and understanding for the first time that eternal life cannot be obtained by keeping religious rules or duties, but simply by putting faith in Jesus. And that is the message of the Gospel, to believe in Jesus.

> JESUS EXPLAINED TO NICODEMUS THAT THIS OLD TESTAMENT EVENT WAS A FORESHADOW OF REDEMPTION FOR ALL WHO HAVE BEEN BITTEN AND LADEN WITH THE VENOM OF SIN

Jesus had made clear the truth that Nicodemus needed to know in order to satisfy the quest of his heart. He revealed to Nicodemus that He is the Son of Man, (the Son of God), and told Nicodemus that He was going to be lifted up on the cross before it happened. So, when Nicodemus saw Jesus on the cross, everything became clear as day to him. He remembered Jesus' words and clearly understood God's plan of redemption.

Did Nicodemus understand this, did he put his faith in Jesus, who was lifted on the cross, did he become Jesus' disciple? Yes, Nicodemus did, because it was Nicodemus and another friend, Joseph of Arimathea, a member of the council, who brought Jesus down from the cross to go and bury Him in Joseph's tomb (John 19:38-40).

> ETERNAL LIFE CANNOT BE OBTAINED BY KEEPING RELIGIOUS RULES OR DUTIES, BUT SIMPLY BY PUTTING FAITH IN JESUS. AND THAT IS THE MESSAGE OF THE GOSPEL, TO BELIEVE IN JESUS.

Jesus on many occasions had preached to several thousands of people and taught them about the Kingdom of Heaven, but here in this private conversation, He revealed this great truth about God's love for the world to one man, an honest and seeking heart, because God is a personal God. He is the God who leaves the ninety-nine sheep, in search of lost one.

From this private conversation comes the most populous verse of the Bible,

"For God so loved the world that He gave His only begotten Son, that whoever believes in Him should not perish but have everlasting life" **(John 3:16).**

This was such a great revelation to Nicodemus; this was very much different from what he had learned. For example, he knew quite well that *"the soul that sins, it shall die"* (Ezekiel 18:4), but Jesus was saying to him that God really does not want anyone to perish but have everlasting life.

To You

Finally, Jesus speaks these words to you, and if you respond to His words, and believe in Him you will find Him to be true to His promises.

*"**Come to Me, all you who labor and are heavy laden, and I will give you rest**"* **(Mathew 11:28).**

*"On the last day, that great day of the feast, Jesus stood and cried out, saying, "**If anyone thirsts, let him come to Me and drink**"* **(John 7:37).**

*"Then Jesus spoke to them again, saying, "**I am the light of the world. He who follows Me shall not walk in darkness but have the light of life**"* **(John 8:12).**

*"31 Then Jesus said to those Jews who believed Him, "If you abide in My word, you are My disciples indeed. 32 **And you shall know the truth, and the truth shall make you free.**" ....36 **Therefore if the Son makes you free, you shall be free indeed**"* **(John 8: 31-32, 36).**

*"**Let not your heart be troubled; you believe in God, believe also in Me**"* **(John 14:1).**

"The thief does not come except to steal, and to kill, and to destroy. **I have come that they may have life, and that they may have it more abundantly"** (John 10:10).

"35 Jesus heard that they had cast him out; and when He had found him, He said to him, **"Do you believe in the Son of God?"** *36 He* **answered and said, "Who is He, Lord, that I may believe in Him?"** *37 And Jesus said to him, "You have both seen Him and it is He who is talking with you."* *38 Then he said, "Lord, I believe!" And he worshiped Him"* (John 9:35-38).

25 *The woman said to Him,* **"I know that Messiah is coming (He who is called Christ—the Anointed);** *when that One comes, He will tell us everything [we need to know]."* 26 **Jesus said to her, "I who speak to you, am He (the Messiah)."** (John 4:25-26 AMP)

John 8:7-12
John 9:35-38
John 11:32-36, 40, 43
John 12:3-7
John 12:7
John 19:26-27
John 20:26-28
Luke 22:31-32
Mark 16:6-7
John 21:15-17
Matthew 26:48-50
Luke 5:20
Luke 7:24-28
Luke 8:45-48
Luke 19:5
John 4:4 KJV
Luke 19:5
Luke 19:10
Luke 23:42-43
John 3:1-4, 14-17
John 12:19
John 3:10 AMP
1 Corinthians 2:14
2 Corinthians 3:6 AMP
Number 21:8
John 3:14-16
John 19:38-40
John 3:16
Ezekiel 18:4
Matthew 11:28
John 7:37
John 8:12
John 8:31-32, 36
John 14:1
John 10:10
John 9:35-38
John 4:25-26 AMP

NOTES

NOTES

ABOUT THE AUTHOR

MICHAEL O. ATUNRASE, SR. Ph.D., is Senior Pastor of Cornerstone Bible Fellowship Church, Levittown, Pennsylvania. His unique way of sharing profound truths is aimed at bringing unbelievers to Christ, and aiding believers toward Christian growth and increasing commitment to Christ. Pastor Atunrase's teaching ministry animates real life with real hope. His depth of spiritual insight and honest reflections about life inspire people around the world to faith, hope, love and joy. His teachings necessitate a disciplined study of the Word of God. A visionary and a missionary, he has traveled extensively, preaching and lecturing and equipping church leaders throughout the United States and around the world, and has studied and demonstrated proficiency in various fields such as theology, education, Christian counseling, writing, speaking and applied sciences, (Biochemistry, Bacteriology and Public Health). Dr. Atunrase is author of *'7Realities The Devil Doesn't want You to Know* "and online daily devotions, *"Daily Refreshing"*. He is President of MOVE-MEN†, an International Ministry to Men and President of Cornerstone International Christian Ministries. A Protestant Minister, for the State of New Jersey, Department of Rehabilitation and is an ordained Bishop with the Association of the Evangelical Gospel Assemblies, USA. He is blessed with his wife Pastor Lola and their children, Michael Jr and Jacqueline, Emily, Sarah, Joshua and grandchildren, Ava-Jade and Michael-James.

For information on speaking, seminars and workshops, contact **Dr. Michael Atunrase, Sr.** at

MOLAT PUBLISHERS
2660 Trenton Road,
Levittown, PA 19056
Email: 7Realitiesdaily@gmail.com

@Bishopmichaelatunrase

MOVE-MENᵗ
Helping Pastors Who Disciples Men
Have A Men's Group? We can Help.
Your men are in for a wonderful encounter with God at a
MOVE-MENᵗ Weekend Retreat.

CONTACT US NOW FOR YOUR NEXT
Men's Outreach Program.
movementretreats@gmail.com

The

MOVE-MENT is an international ministry aimed at empowering Men for their placements in the Kingdom, by providing Leadership, Mentoring, Discipleship, Fellowship, Ministry, Networking, Peering, and opportunity for Global Missions. It is a ministry for men with hearts after God who desire to merge action with passion in their pursuit of a closer walk with God. The ministry is designed to promote fellowship among godly men and to encourage them in their Journey of Biblical Manhood.

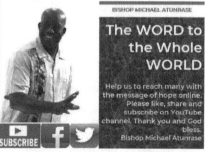

https://www.youtube.com/@BishopMICHAELATUNRASE

Made in the USA
Columbia, SC
15 September 2023

22882410R00067